THE PAINT OF INVENTION

by

The artist Jack Priest

The Paint of Invention
by The artist Jack Priest, 1st ed.

Contents

Acknowledgments

Having lived a long life and faced many of life's challenges, I believe what I have learned and experienced have made me the person I am today. I don't believe I'm an exceptional person, talented or learned. What I am is a person who has tried to live a decent life and added to the human condition in many positive ways, silently and without recognition. Yes, I have had many people dislike me, and some may have even hated me for a whatever reason. I don't believe anyone can escape that in their lives. Life is not easy living in a society; we just have to make the best of our existence.

Sometimes we meet very good people, thus, I want to thank EJ Pollard and Kathleen Weisel for all their help to accomplish this book.

Everything has a language. Whether you're learning a spoken language or how to be a doctor, the task is laborious. It is difficult to learn any language much less four, five or ten; few of us can do that.

What if we create a universal language which can be used to communicate with anyone on the planet using the fundamentals we all have.

chapter one

THE FREEDOM "IN" ART

Never assume what an artist is trying to say in a work of art; view it, and if you're intrigued, then ask, "What is the work of art trying to tell me?" You see, it's all about you, the viewer.

Most people are in a relaxed mode when they go to a museum or a gallery and they're not looking at paintings to analyze them. So, what are they looking for? Why are they at an art venue? What is the experience of being exposed to an artistic creation? The simple answer is: They want to learn and absorb something that resonates in the heart and soul. The desire to find emotions that someone else sees and feels is compelling. Like all aspects of human endeavor, art has many meanings for creators and viewers, so the answer may never be as simple as fulfilling the need of a viewer.

Knowing the intent of an artist and the language they have used is as important as being exposed to the creation itself. There are hundreds of styles, schools of art, and movements; when combined, result in art as we know it. These, individually and collectively, make art difficult to understand. As you pass works of art in a gallery searching for a connection and you haven't seen a glimpse of what may arouse feelings within you, maybe you look for the artist statement to read what they had in mind, and then try to understand the meaning. Maybe you ask yourself if the world has left you behind. Perhaps your expectations are beyond reasonable. Possibly, as a viewer, you may not think about it at all. You still don't get it, and you move on to the next work of art. You have said more about the art by a lack of interest than the artist has displayed in the creation. This is a normal reaction, because human beings are a unique species; we are all looking for a connection we're comfortable with. Some people would say a portrait of a dog may be just what we're looking for.

———•———

The art world is a reflection of everything in humanity and society. And thus, it is necessary to include some of the challenges an artist has to face and understand. In recent years many robberies have taken place that appear to fit the "stolen to order" bill. The break-ins at museums and private residences around the world appear to target specific art works of high value. Some of these artworks are destroyed and others disappear for years. You might think an act like this would never occur; in truth, it has happened countless times throughout history, and is taking place as we speak.

Acts have also been carried out to erase history. In 2001, the Taliban of Afghanistan decided to demolish the colossal Buddhas of Bamiyan (that had existed for 1500 years), because the Muslim government declared they were idols and against the teachings of the Quran. The destruction was viewed by the rest of the world as an example of the extreme intolerance of the Buddhist religion by the Muslim Taliban, (Buddhists today are only .01% of the population in Afghanistan.) Also, ISIS jihadists (the Islamic State of Iraq and Syria group of militants), readily destroyed such ancient Greco-Roman wonders as the Temple of Bel, the Temple of Baalshamin, the Arch of Triumph and columns in the Valley of the Tombs in Syria's historic town of Palmyra (a UNESCO World Heritage Site) claiming cultural cleansing.

Appropriation of history to suit a narrative and to destroy the art of earlier times, is like burning your birth certificate and then saying you never had parents because there is no proof you were ever born.

There is a lesson to be learned in these behaviors and the answer is in the form of a question: If you destroy history, will there be history to replace it? The answer is simple: If you destroy history, there is no history that can replace it because you just destroyed it.

What you've been reading points to the complicated forces constantly at play that will open your mind to a whole new world you have to understand. And, we will reveal stronger movements trying to manipulate you. (Trends you will have to pay attention to.)

———•———

We now find it necessary to define everything because we are faced with many contradictions and competing agendas. Finding emotions inside of you that someone else sees and feels appears to be an easy answer. Something else has to happen to ignite those feelings and make explosions happen in the emotions of the viewer.

For the artist, wanting to go somewhere, or do something, is not sufficient enough reason to do it. The only bond the artist can achieve is a connection with the viewer, sometimes this happens, and sometimes it doesn't. If you find yourself frustrated when going to an art venue, reading the words on these pages will give you a new perspective.

"This is a living book."

There is an art language to be found. You'll be reading about gaining more from what you see, and acquiring the ability to exercise what you've learned, whether you consider yourself an artist or a person who appreciates viewing art. We're going to follow a course of explanation that embodies the closest meaning of these intentions. The narrative and examples you read are purely informative, and they will be your guide to a stronger understanding of art and its principles.

We will explore the three segments of an artist's progression: the beginning, the middle, and the end result. The first step is formulating your plan and doing the actual work of putting your plan and technique into motion. The middle is getting your promotion plan together, and finally, introducing your work into the competition of the open arena.

You will find blank pages and empty space throughout this book; they are there so you will have a place to write your personal observations. This is a living book and your notes will always be together so you might reference them at a later date. I suggest you read through the book first and then write your thoughts; since many aspects of art overlap and do not remain on topic. You will find similar subjects discussed and statements made in multiple chapters. I say this because: if you write a question about what has been said and then later read the answer you may feel put off, and we certainly don't want that to happen. In fact, record all your comments in pencil, that way if a mistake does happen you can erase it.

With simple tools and knowledge at your disposal, you will have the ability to attach reason and understanding to the subject of art. Since freedom can be as much of a burden as the thoughts and practices you are trying to free; there are parameters with different meanings and responsibilities each of us have to learn. Drawings and pictures are excluded from this book on purpose, they'll have to be created in your mind. Since the beginning of all art is metaphysical (with no basis in reality) we will be building and developing art as an abstract concept. We will be using the principles of the Freedom in Art, as an invention with guidelines and controls. The practice is about applying knowledge, which is what gets exercised before any action takes place, whether as a creator of art, or as a viewer of art.

With millions of creators and people who appreciate art having lived before this time, the odds are almost certain what I'm going to share with you has been said before. Therefore, I am going to be concise and limit my examples, and explanations, as close to the essentials as possible. People read in different ways; do not think there is anything to learn by reading between the lines, or that there are double-entendres to discover because there aren't any. This book is about art and nothing more. It may be that you have to read portions over and over again to understand what has been said; but, it is better to have repetition than to read examples that lead you in various directions and leave a question mark in your mind. Also, be aware, there are always exceptions to every rule.

If you are looking to have a hobby, or using art as therapy, this book may not be for you. Since, the very nature of delving deeply into understanding art, where it is and its future is intensely provoking. You're looking to build on the thinking and spirit that makes art the most potent influence mankind has ever known.

Since we are starting at the beginning, I'll share some reflections that may sound simplistic, and possibly fatalistic. It's not as bad as it might sound. In fact, it's definitely where the door opens to the next adventure.

chapter two

LET'S OPEN THE DOOR

I have to settle an issue so it is easy to understand, and that's the rolls played by the artist, and the viewer. Both are embodied in every individual. The only difference is how they are looked upon and understood in a given time and place. If this statement means to control our performance in a certain way; I will say yes. To be more exact, each of us has to compartmentalize our performances. It is the way we act and react as an artist and as a viewer individually. An entire book can be written on this subject alone because there are many, many definitions for the words behavior, performance and act. I have only chosen these words because I believe they are the closest in meaning to get our point across. Also, when I refer to an artist, I am speaking of the practicing artist and to the singular nature, not the dual nature of the individual. The viewer in the compartment can be anyone without qualification. However, there is a separation between a viewer and a critic, which we will talk about later. Keep in mind what I just said and let's move on.

Art does not stand alone; it is the expression or application of creative skill and imagination by an inventor, which then must be acknowledged by a viewer. The artist and viewer are equal partners in the experience of art. Humanity has the ability to separate the two for the sake of academics, but, that does not change the true meaning and value of art.

"Great art is chosen by viewers."

There's a tantalizing question I often hear, and that question is: "What is art?" This issue seems to befuddle everybody. Art is involved with every endeavor of human existence. Simply put, anything that's not procreating or supporting is art, which later can be, or evolve, into craft. I realize this explanation sounds broad, however everything has a beginning, and that beginning is called art, whether it was first expressed ten generations ago or yesterday.

The next question is the goodie. "What is good art?" The answer is held in the eyes of the beholder. The artist Paul Cezanne is considered the father of Modern Art, and credited with being an influence to many great artists. Each one of those artists painted differently. How would you account for that? Each of those artists saw the same colors, the same planes, and the same lines. The "beholders" were looking for technique, and they all saw it in a different way. Thus, the "same but different" principle applies. How many faces do you have to see, for you to agree they are all faces, and they're all different?

Let's keep going with the flow. "What is great art?" Without hesitation, it's art that touches the identity of a people. Many works of art that affect different emotions in large numbers of people, become great art. When a work of art evokes many feelings, such as sorrow, love, heroism and tenderness, at the right time, and in the right place, it is open to becoming great art, but only if it is chosen.

All art is good, and lives in a constant state of upset in its attempt to find a path into the future because few of us think alike and have the same knowledge and understanding. Many artists and viewers of art believe nobody knows what art is, or is not. Thus, outside forces or spheres of influence are left to determine an identity for much of the contemporary art world, whether it is valid or not. When there is doubt about the validity of anything, confusion becomes the byproduct.

Stepping aside for a moment, let's list words that are important to this conversation:

Invention means:
Origination, creation, innovation, discovery, design, devising, contriving, coining, construction, inventiveness, originality, creativity, imagination, artistry, inspiration, ingenuity, fabrication, concoction, fiction, falsification, forgery, fake, deceit, myth, fantasy, romance, illusion, sham, lie, untruth, falsehood, fib, piece of fiction, figment of ones imagination, yarn or story.

Inventor means:
Originator, creator, discoverer, author, architect, designer, devisor, developer, initiator, coiner, prime mover, maker, framer or producer.

These words have different meanings to artists and viewers of art. This is why we have to define the processes used in the creations we will talk about. Truth means accuracy and correctness. In art, all these words are truths. Again, consider the words "in the eyes of the beholder." We may not use all of these descriptive words, however, all of them are available when discussing art.

Confusion is common in the meaning of words in the field of art, because we are all human and organic in our feelings and emotions. Changing the use of the word "creation" to "design" makes a tremendous difference in the description of graphic art and architecture, yet both use lines and planes put together to achieve a picture. So, the word invention is universal.

Walking in the midst of artistic confusion, it would be nice to only be where our work were on display. That will rarely be the case, so to avoid consternation and dislike, we ignore all that is not ours or to our liking. We balance on a thin line and hope success will keep us from falling off.

Before we move on, let's consider Outsider and Insider art. You are an Outsider if you have no training in the essentials of art and you do everything without forethought (seat of the pants). As an Insider, you will have had an education or training in art history and practice. For us, whether you are self-taught, or have a degree in art, does not matter as long as you have the willingness to learn and apply knowledge.

Art has a special place in our existence because it documents the feelings and emotions of people at certain times in history and acts as the stepping stones to document who and what we are. Humans didn't travel to different areas of the planet without planning, development and action. Everything had to be created and decided upon, to exist as necessary, and useful. What we know as art was the spirit within these people to say, "I am here and I matter."

We are dreamers who have desires for a better world. A few of us will punch a hole in our bubble of a world and guide many to a new way of looking at us, what we have achieved and where we might be in the future. Those ideals are what we strive for through our inventive minds. The reality of dreaming is only as useful as the knowledge and tools we have available to achieve those goals.

Being an inventor means we are responsible to create tools to attain the lofty goals we have set for ourselves. That's really where art lives.

chapter three

APPLY THE FIVE Ws TO ART

Who:
Art is the unconditional expression of the freedom to think what you want to think, and go where you want to go, without restraint, or restriction. It's the thought and spirit that makes everything come alive.

What:
Art, can be whatever you want it to be, and what space you want it to occupy. You, as a creator of art, are the person to decide what will inhabit an area of space. You can add an action or a motive, it is up to you.

When:
Art has no timeline. It may be in the past, present or future. Or, it may be in any dimension you choose. Art may be in any combination of time and space.

Where:
Art can take place anywhere your mind decides, from the molecular to the outer reaches of the universe and beyond.

Why:
The artist decides what lives, what they want to exist or represent, how useful the art will be, or will not be, in what context, and, in what aspect of our existence the creation lives. Similar to writing a story in dimensions, the narrative may be broken up in any way the artist desires to display a purpose and reason for being.

The Five Ws you have just read have to have parameters because none of us live in a vacuum. The freedom to imagine, to aspire; the freedom of expression and the freedom of art have no inherent controls and allow speech and actions without fact or reason. Make note to understand the freedom you have; by looking at both sides of everything, you have the control to decide which way to go and what needs to be done to make it reasonable. As you read further, we will address many of the boundaries that have to be acknowledged.

An invention will always be pushed by many sides to fit in a place where it will be comfortable and workable. Imagine filling a balloon with water and then trying to fit it into an empty water glass. You push on one side and the other side bulges out; you have to continue molding and adding pressures to sides until you are able to get the balloon into the glass. This is what any original creation has to go through to meet the parameters of a composition, to make an impact on the viewer.

The Five Ws are the backbone of the Freedom in Art, and it is essential to constantly be aware of their existence. It does no good to put together a story that has conflicting facts that will have to be explained in detail taking you away from the story you are trying to tell.

"Art is inherently unstable and irrational, that's why we need controls. Orville and Wilbur Wright knew the dynamics of flight needed controls to make an AIRPLANE work. Without controls to direct airflow an airplane will never fly."

chapter four

THE POWER OF IMAGES

Before putting brush and paint together, we have to think ahead and create a narrative. Having made this statement, many artists say they prefer to put paint to canvas and allow the result to dictate when to advance to the next step. Jumping into the process (without a plan), the artist feels they are one with art, and in partnership with the canvas and tools, foregoing the thinking process. The artist also feels like they are on the verge of discovery every time they enter this state of mind.

This is not a laughing matter; most artists have experienced this exact frame of mind. We all understand whole-heartedly what they're saying. You have to believe the mental outcome from this practice is outstanding, and it certainly gives you a positive mindset. You are one with a higher power, and in a state of euphoria. Many artists who are talent driven believe this is the only qualification. They believe they are guided by an unknown force that is spiritual in nature and beyond their control and consciousness.

This way of thinking about art is called "seat-of-the-pants," because it is skipping the most important step on the path to an end result; we have to begin with a plan and a map to get to our goal. You have to know what you're trying to achieve and the reason why you are doing it. The goal becomes your subject, and the story becomes the map to get you there. You won't be looking to discover a reason for your creation's existence. Your story points to the end result; and, you'll achieve a lot more if you plan how to get there.

Getting started is easy, the most advantageous subject matter for beginners is to think of a story you already know, and then relate that to an artistic creation. For those more accomplished, and well-read, think directly of a subject you want to delve into, and create a story. The story can be anything: a fairy tale, a myth, a lie, a real world report, are a few examples. A story doesn't exist by itself; it can be composed around any subject. It must be believable to qualify, even if it is the biggest lie you have ever told.

———◆-◆-◆———

Having had a conversation with an artist at a gallery where he had several of his paintings displayed, the artist began to explain one of his pictures. He talked about the strength of his lines, and the voluptuous color he used, with strong brush strokes, and how it all emotionally came out of him to splatter on the canvas. He said it was a part of him that was causing pain and he had to get it out. Listening intently for him to give more detail (after all, he did gain our attention), he didn't explain the painting further. An artist statement was not to be found. The painting did not have a goal and didn't have a story, only snippets of emotion. What we heard did not have credibility. Contrary to what some people believe, the goal of art is not about the artist, it's about what the viewer sees in the creation.

So, you are the maker of your destiny. Is your intent to create art in the image of art you identify with, the art you like the most, and are eager to emulate? You can do that if you want to, it's your call. I have said many times that all art is good art (the qualifier), and we all have different needs to fulfill. If you are looking to advance art, whatever your story may be, it must go in a forward motion. Every story has a past, a present and a future; it also has a beginning, a middle and an end. Each story should be objective. Knowing these facts, you must use a system to further your art as you see fit. Never forgetting the principles of balance, emphasis, movement, proportion, rhythm, unity, and variety to organize elements within, to give it equilibrium and stability.

Ask yourself these questions:
- Who is the subject of the painting?
- What is the subject matter of the painting?
- What is the subject doing?
- What is the subject trying to tell the viewer?
- What happens, or has happened, to compel the viewer to see the story?
- When is the action taking place?
- Where is the action taking place?
- What will be the artist's universal truth toward the subject?
- With what universal truth do you expect the viewer to identify with?

All artists are organic dreamers. However, nobody goes to sleep thinking they will solve a problem in the middle of the night and they will wake up and write the answer down, and then go back to sleep. How magical that would be. But, you can write a story about that happening and play to dreams as if they were real and put together all the facts to justify it.

"There is a love that permeates you when everything is in balance; it doesn't matter what the subject is."

chapter five

THE MIND'S EYE AND BASIC UNDERSTANDING

The view we see with our eyes is not exactly the true vision we behold; it's a combination of imprinting, training, knowledge, desire and reality. The narrative we relate to will always be different, in some respect, than that of others. The sum of the relative facts of who and what you are is reflected in the vision you see. Everyone has experienced two different stories of the same vision. Since truth is in the eyes of the beholder, and no other, this does not mean you will never be able to make a connection with a viewer. The mind's eye is the mental picture which you have conceived.

The inventor is the one telling the story through their vision and art. Life is made up of the real and the abstract, so it is not out of context to visualize in the abstract or in what is real. We all play different roles in life, and as an inventor, we give identity to our creations so they will take on a personality and come alive. Subject matter is primary and all the shapes of a character tell your mind it has real behavior even though you might be looking at a cartoon. The reality factor tells you it is fiction. In this way we can identify with a viewer and make an emotional connection.

From a viewer's point of view:

The viewer is the first party, the creation takes on the identity of the second party, and the inventor is the third party. The viewer always comes first, since the whole purpose of creating art is to connect with a viewer. We, the inventors, would all like to think of ourselves as the most important part of this arrangement, but we are not. From the artist's point of view: Every creation should begin in the mind as a vision; starting with a goal using the Five Ws, through the process of planning the work of art, and finally to completion. It is true, the artist is the only person within this moment. However, the first person identity must be transferred to the creation and then to the viewer to be successful. This action completes the bonding circle.

———◆———

Every work of art has something of a story. On the other hand, not every work of art is a complete story. We've all seen art showing one side of what could be a many-sided story. Often, you may have to rush to the side of an artwork to read what the artist has written to know the rest of the story.

There's something more to think about in a work of art, regardless of the subject or technique, and that's time. When you read a book, it might take you ten hours of reading if you read it straight through, or, ten days if you read one hour a day. Whichever way you read, it's taken ten hours to come to the conclusion of the story. If you watch a movie that's two hours long, it'll take that long to get to the conclusion. When you listen to a song or a tune, you have maybe three or four minutes to understand what you've heard and decide whether you like it or not. With most visual art, you have one minute or less, to convey your whole story. The artist has to uniquely relate who, what, when, where, and why to interest the viewer in under one minute! The work of art becomes the first person telling the story. This can be an exhilarating experience for the viewer who then accepts the first party roll; it makes the viewer feel like the first person to play a part in its discovery. Imagine going to an art show and viewing twenty or thirty fabulous stories in an hour.

"Few of us wake up when we're 10 years old and start painting like Rembrandt at age 60."

Human beings are internally driven toward art as necessary to the human condition. Naturally, there are two conditions outside of art that dominate the greater part of our lives: procreating and supporting. There's a good reason why people have hobbies or outside interests; to keep them creatively involved during their years of responsibility.

All art has a development period. It took decades and thousands of people to develop the smart phone and all those people had to go through the education and development stages. For the artist, understanding the process, science, and acceptance, will lead to solutions for what will become the foundation, and then the creation of art.

When we talk about the Freedom in Art, maneuvering around preconditions to be able to say you're free as an artist is not easy to understand. The key to this is to look at all aspects differently; preconditions are part of the tools of your art, as much as the paint, canvas and brushes you may use to create. These conditions can be altered in whatever way makes you happy. The easy part is mixing and matching paints, choosing brushes, or, tacking a large canvas to a wall. After you create your work of art, you can decide what space you want the art to live in. Your state of mind is the freedom you have, and you get to decide where it begins and where it ends.

Many artists who've come before us have exercised their freedom until they decide to stop, and often they're then said to have found their style. How many dimensions you want to travel in, and how long you want your journey to last, is what makes you a better artist.

We all want to know about the containment of the spirit within us. The freedom you possess has no boundaries. We know the limits we'll travel and feel safe. Often, this is where we'll contain ourselves. But, you don't have to stop there, the human spirit can soar to infinity and beyond, and you can create the time and space you desire through your mind's eye. It is true some people are more accomplished in doing this than others; practice does make you better.

Discovery is weak on its own; you have to know what you're looking for to be able to recognize it when you see it. That fact doesn't mean you should look for only one discovery, you should be scanning all areas of your art. When you find a glimmer that fits your criteria, then focus in on it. Remember all the great artists who credit Paul Cezanne as an influence in their art? They all discovered something different. The more you question and learn, the more you will discover.

⸻◦⸻

Early on, we said great art is something that touches the identity of a people. If you speak English and people of another country speak a different language, but love and identify with your art, you must have used a language understood by those viewers to be able to communicate with them. You tell the story in your art and they're able to read it through their mind's eye; thus making the language of art universal. Not everyone who looks at a painting can interpret it. It does take time and practice for many viewers to be able to see the language through their mind's eye.

Without appearing academic, the mind's eye can read a good story rapidly without having to interpret every nuance. It is done by recognizing universal truths. I'm sure you've seen documentaries about ducks and geese who are imprinted to a human, people make similar imprints. We can recognize the face of someone we know out of hundreds of pictures. We know what a person is doing when we see a picture of someone kneeling in front of a church alter; or a man lying in a mud hole with a helmet on and a rifle at his side. These are universal truths most adults can recognize and read immediately, no matter what their spoken language is.

The mind also recognizes order; we know where the sky is, where the sun and moon are, and the earth beneath our feet. We know danger and when to fight or run. We also know the order of plants and animals. We know trees have a main trunk with limbs growing out from the trunk, and dogs have a head in front where their eyes, nose and mouth are. We can recognize all these shapes when we see them mixed up in a picture. So, the mind's eye seeks order using knowledge. This is important, because order is the key to both memory and universal truths.

All our senses are connected. Your mind can hear sounds associated with visuals; it can feel an explosion in a photograph, or know the fragrance of a beautiful rose shown in a painting. You can say these are connected influences. Have you ever not wanted to pet a cute puppy that's playing around your feet?

During the era of silent films, viewers could experience all the senses in a movie through their mind's eye. Perhaps the only reason they had an organ player was to add tension and drama, to make it an exciting experience.

chapter six

INFLUENCES

Since the art world spans such a broad spectrum, borders are left unchecked, leaving room for influence from outside sources.

The most extreme parameters are involved for you to have the basic knowledge and understanding of influence. Humans exist in a realm of uncertainty. It is a competitive world from the day we start associating with others until we die; everyone has wants and needs, and develops an agenda. Art is about creation not about the creator of art.

This is where the Freedom in Art must stand on its principles. There's no justification to talk about the Freedom in Art unless we speak of the inner organic influences; those which we can't control or change but can ignore, and outer influences which can be created, changed, manipulated and discarded, as well as being ignored. As an artist you can be under the influence of an agenda as well as being able to exert an influence.

The foundation of the Freedom in Art is fundamental. It does have limitations keeping it focused on art. Recognizing that inner influences guide and mold art in an objective way. The challenge for an artist believing in the Freedom "IN" Art is to limit as many outside influences as possible. Although, outside influence as a subject is acceptable.

The freedom within you is a concept of the mind, and contains some minor qualities of perception and rejection. The genes you were born with will not change, but the perception of who and what you are may be changed, even if you appear to remain the same person. Put yourself in the mind of an actor and you'll know what I'm talking about.

Influences have to be recognized; you have to come to terms with their reality and be able to free yourself to overcome those pressures, no matter how they are perceived. Some influences are easily discarded, and others are so difficult you'll have to change the concept of self to conquer them. We're not saying to give up and go with the flow; instead we're saying to recognize all the facts and make appropriate decisions while keeping your artistic goal in mind. You are the master of thinking. Accepting influences is important to be able to rid yourself of them, control them, or at least modify them to fit your own needs and the needs of your audience.

By releasing influences you become the universal artist who speaks in only one language, the language of art. You become the creator using any tools at your disposal in the name of invention.

We can state categorically, the Freedom in Art knows no division within the artist. The tools of the artist, be they paints and brushes, or chisels and hammers, do not know who or what the artist is or is not.

If you see a painting you like, and you're later told it was painted by an elephant at the zoo, does that change the beauty of the painting? Certainly not! The painting and it's reason for being stands on its own, even if it is non-objective. There's only a problem if you are told it is exceptional art because it was painted by an elephant; taking away your judgment as a viewer.

Your ability to create stands on the freedom to use knowledge as an artist without detrimental influences of an inner or outer nature. If the Freedom in Art is allowed to be tainted by detrimental influences outside of the subject matter, it's no longer free; not for the artist, and not for the viewer.

Like all endeavors with the same influence, when they compete with one another and mimic each other's practices, they tend to nullify their potential. Rather than relying on individuality and quality, these pressures work to divide artists and viewers, and to confuse the value of an artistic creation. Events such as this have happened in many of the arts. This works on some individuals for a while but the effect appears to be fleeting. For the artist, adopting the Freedom in Art has to take the place of who you are, ridding yourself of influences. Artists surround themselves with the boundaries they willingly choose. This may change from one work of art to the next, and artists must devote themselves to the demands of each.

Art is not limited by being stripped of its influences; it is being stripped down to the truth and prepared for presentation.

chapter seven

YOUR AUDIENCE

Identity has a real impact on you as an artist, and what it means to your audience. The freedom experienced has no meaning for the artist unless someone else is there to recognize it. You have to pay attention to your position, and the status of the viewer. As the artist, you can create anything you want and you can question your motives. The ultimate goal is to be able to have a universal conversation with your audience.

Ask any child who they are, and they'll probably tell you their name. Ask the child what they are, and they'll tell you something just as simple. Does that change the fact they are a precious part of humanity? Or maybe, they are in the beginning stages of developing into one of the greatest minds of our time? The questions may always be the same; the answers become much more complex as we develop and age. Our scope of life has many facets, and the artist must pay attention to those characteristics in order to engage the audience in partnership.

We have said the following questions need to be answered: "What is the experience of being exposed to the artistic creation?" And, "Am I learning and absorbing something that resonates in the heart and soul?" The desire of an audience to find expressions within your art that they may see and feel is compelling. Yes, art can be anything you want it to be: beautiful, ugly, funny, assaulting, shocking. Sometimes, the most unique and original art can languish and turn viewers away. Few people will want to see it, and your art is dead because it doesn't have an audience. Art has to be a pleasant experience or a provocative one, or both. It has to be in the right time and place to get the greatest audience. Vincent van Gogh is the perfect example of an artist who produced revolutionary art ahead of the time and place when it would be accepted.

"The Impressionists and the Fauves liked the idea of creating new art and attracting viewers."

There are two ways an artist can look at their work when considering audience: presenting art to appeal to a specific demographic of viewer, or, moving a target audience to the art. Venues prefer the "presenting approach" whereas artists much prefer (or are subject to) the "creating an audience approach." The Impressionists and the Fauves liked the idea of creating new art and attracting viewers with a different perspective of their work. When venues finally took notice of their success, they changed their attitudes to take advantage of this new art to bring a contemporary audience to their venues. Success of the new art made it possible for venues to move the art from the "creating an audience approach" to their "presenting approach."

In art, the fewer facts you have in your creation, the fewer people will find an interest in it. The quality and universal nature of your facts play a role in the acceptance as well. If you're looking for an audience between the ages of six and ten, the universal facts must be understood by that age group. If the audience you're seeking are people between the ages of 20 and 35, and grew up loving movies about outer space, you'll be seeking multi-faceted universal facts. And, you'll have to make adjustments in how those will be portrayed to appeal to this new audience.

Let's delve into this subject further; say you're creating an exhibition about outer space. The first question would more than likely be what you want to achieve with the show or what you want to exhibit. Then, who or what you'll spotlight. You'll want to put it in a time period and where in space it will be. Then explain why all these events are happening. You have many choices, and you'll have to focus on the needs of the audience. It does not matter in what order these thoughts arise in your first vision, or, whether they are repeated or not. What matters is the Five Ws are there to be found and later to be organized.

If your audience is young, with little historical knowledge about real outer space programs. They may not understand what science and the space program have achieved, who the heroes were, the equipment they used or the reasons for the programs they were in; which play a part in the story. These young people grow up with outside influences, that can be hypothetical, fanciful, and full of conflict. Often involving a lot of drama, aliens, and fantasy. For this younger audience, it might be a better choice to put together video clips that tell a story about space and wars between planets in the galaxy as your audience is used to seeing it. Using movie props interspersed with actual space artifacts with sound and music, creating a vision of space they can recognize. You're playing to people excited about the future, and all the possibilities of a new world and a great adventure. Of course, care must be taken to inform your audience of what is real and what is "show business."

For an exhibit about outer space to attract an older audience, the best plan may be exhibiting models of space capsules, parts of rockets, photographs of astronauts in space, clips of news stories, rocks from the moon and the real every-day results those early flights achieved. In this scenario, the exhibit might be of great interest to a generation who experienced those early days of the space program, when it was an opening item in the news.

As you have just read, an artist's goals are not unlike the goals of a curator at a museum; the Five Ws have to be there and you have to consider your audience. Knowing they can only bring you closer to the target you want to make a connection with, whether it already exists or the one you will bring together.

———◆———

Most artists spend much of their time thinking about the tools they need to accomplish what they want to do on a canvas. The tools are important, but you have to know there is a place for everything in your plan for success. The difference is in what you want and what the viewer wants. If you want to get a driver's license, it would be wise to find out what the DMV expects you to know before attempting the written test and then the driver's test. In the end, it's not about the tools to make a car, it's about how to drive the car to get the drivers license you need.

No matter what your work looks like, never allow the vulgar and commonplace dominate its identity; if you do, you'll effectively create an issue to overcome and diminish the spirit of what you've created.

Here are a few last thoughts we have to think about when we consider audience. There are billions of people on earth who are potential admirers. If all of them know about your art and want to see it, you would be more successful than any artist in history. Being realistic, to be a success, would you have to have 1,000 admirers, 10,000 admirers, or maybe a million? Nobody knows because there are so many different scenarios you can concoct with different numbers. Truly, an audience always starts with one admirer, and that's all you need to know.

chapter eight

TRAGEDY

Depictions of conflict were common in the time when government and religion dictated content to artist/craftsmen. Today, tragedies are not a popular subject for many artists because there are many facets in the subject where emotions dominate. You have to decide what your story will champion, and the compelling reason for creating a work of art. Are you going to make a statement? Are you going to glorify the tragedy? Will you show sympathy for those left behind when their loved ones die?

Let's write a war story:

A shell-shocked soldier is staggering through debris from a battle; head turned back aimlessly facing toward the sky. He's dragging his rifle by the shoulder strap and flailing the air in front of him with his free hand. A half naked child is in front of him, dirty and crying, his mother lying dead at his feet, bombs exploding around the group. A sign lying on the ground reads, "Freedom for the People!" *The compelling story: War is horrific for everyone involved whether they agree with the reason why it's taking place or not.*

This story has all the Five Ws to create a work of art. There are several options using these characters. We have to decide on what the most compelling story would be in the painting. Start with the lead character: is it going to be the shell-shocked young soldier, the half-naked child, the dead mother, or the sign laying on the ground? All of these characters have a good story to tell. We already have the first scenario, so let's write a story for each of the other possibilities, using the "same but different" principle and spotlighting a leading character with a different compelling reason.

This is what we get:

A child, half naked, cries furiously for the security of his mother's breast, alone in the midst of the catastrophe of war. His mother lies dead on the ground next to him. A shell-shocked soldier passes by, not knowing where he is. The cry for freedom banner lies on the ground, bloody and in tatters. All is lost, and the war rages in the background. *The compelling story: Children are the victims in every war.*

Next:

A woman lay dead on the ground. She can no longer protect the child she brought into the world and nurtured. The child is devastated, not knowing what has happened. Bombs are exploding with horrific noise, and shock waves fill the air. Not even the soldier with a rifle can help him. The banner for which she stood lay next to her. *The compelling story: Mothers want a better world for their children and they're willing to give up their lives to get it.*

And finally:

The banner becomes the spotlight character reading, "Freedom for the People!" It lies on the battlefield, bloodied and torn, being clutched by a dead woman. A half naked child is crying furiously next to the woman, who is obviously his mother. A shell-shocked soldier stumbles by, aimlessly dragging his rifle, having given up the fight. Bombs explode in the background. *The compelling story: Freedom has tremendous value and is worth fighting for. Sometimes, there's a price to pay in human suffering and loss of life.*

It's easy to see how the same basics can be used to come up with different stories by spotlighting or creating a principle character. The Freedom in Art makes it possible to create something that will encompass your passion and commitment. Each of these four stories are fascinating, and the choice you make is the one you feel most comfortable with.

⟺⟹

Let's shift gears and address the subject of tragedy, which in the minds of many, is just as gripping as the depiction of war because the same feelings and emotions are at play.

Just so you know: War, conflict and tragedy are bundled together because they are all part of the tragedy label. You can call war a conflict and you can label a conflict a tragedy.

We can start anywhere in a story to put together the facts. Let's consider a hero, an action, a place where the action takes place, a timeline, and the reason for an event happening. Anything that comes to mind can be our pivot point.

Let's put a story together:

Today in the newspaper, there was an article about an old historical library in the downtown area falling down during a tremor. There were people inside and walking on the sidewalk at the time of the event. Someone called for help; paramedics and the fire department arrived on the scene within minutes. Every able bodied person in the vicinity came to the scene and moved debris. One of the rescued women said her daughter was missing, and she could hear her voice. The men sprung into action, removing more debris to rescue the little girl who was safe and sound, despite being dirty and shaken. The paramedic who brought her out of the debris handed her over to her crying mother.

Do you see what we have here? We've got a story that can be put on canvas. The hero in this situation is the paramedic, and despite the tragedy of a historical building falling down during an earthquake, nobody died and a young girl was saved. The date on a part of the building that fell down was 1900. The paramedic was dirty and sweaty but happy as he held the girl out toward her crying mother, who was reaching for her daughter. Now, you know the rest of the story.

The most important step is creating a workable story. You have to determine how you want to express the narrative and translate it into a work of art. Then, you must decide what materials you want to use and what measurements would be best to tell the story for the greatest impact on the viewer. The most challenging aspect will be the technique you use. How you translate a story is up to you.

Are we finished yet? Maybe not, if something doesn't fit properly in your mind, think about the people and the actions that can be changed, while still retaining the drama within the story. If you don't feel comfortable rendering a story to a completed canvas right away, file it. Later, you may read these stories and find great contrast to what you are doing in the present and decide to use them for new works of art.

This opens great possibilities for you to exercise your artistic discretion and create a story by asking questions. What if it was a fire instead of a tremor? What if it was caused by a homeless man trying to keep warm? What if it was at night? What if the homeless man rescued a lady and her dog and the lady was in a wheelchair? What if the police and fire department showed up and there was an argument about whether the homeless man should be arrested or given a medal? Every good story can be an even better story when you ask "what if" questions. Try working on two or three ideas a day just to see what you come up with.

chapter nine

IS IT ART OR CRAFT?

Craft is another form of creation having parameters that have to be followed. The only difference is who decides its identity and reproduction. Most often the artist is working at the will of other people, who dictate the content and parameters. The resulting creation will not be qualified by the artist. Often, a commercial creation may be adjusted by numerous artists with specific influences. A television show may have numerous writers working in collaboration with one another. One writer may create the jokes, another writes situations, and maybe there's someone who adds drama. Some TV series have a stable of writers to add their specialties that an episode may require.

Commercial art is a craft and the most copied and repeated form of art. It is not practical to say it's an inferior art, as many do. Art merely becomes something else the more it is commercialized.

Some people believe art is created through the expression of emotions and craft is a form of work which results in a tangible output. If only one item is made by a craftsman, would it not be art using the same process as an artist? Both art and craft have many of the same attributes, but different goals to achieve. An artist is creating a one-of-a-kind work of art, originating in the mind in a free form seeking discovery. A craftsman arranges a planned composition calculated to result in a work that may be reproduced mechanically numerous times with the same result. If an artist creates an original work of art that is later used to make numerous prints, the original is art and the copies are craft. Most often, art is followed by craft and occasionally craft is followed by art. The lesson to be learned is that art has spirit and craft has a plan to sell a commercial product.

Art is transformed into craft when it is influenced by repetition, mechanization or lack of subsequent originality.

A good example is transportation:

Horses were replaced by the train, and trains developed beyond personal conveyance. Other forms of transportation developed to fill niches that could not be serviced by the train. Speeds increased, and the train was eclipsed by the airplane and the automobile, which took over the transportation of people for long distance trips and door to door travel. No matter how beautiful and comfortable the train had become, speed and convenience made it an outmoded form of personal transportation. The automobile and airplane replaced and relegated the train to a form of craft.

Is craftsmanship art? All artistic creations are subject to transformation and becoming craft. If a person spends years creating a few paintings so perfect in line and plane that they appear they were made by a machine; if perfection of technique were the goal, the inventor would certainly succeed. However, what is created is pure craft. Many artists could supersede this person with speed, and create similar artistic works that would be much more spontaneous and alive. Art is about creativity, not perfection.

If you were a painter and decided to make multiple copies from an original creation using the same subject and technique in every copy, the first painting would be the artistic original, and subsequent paintings would be synthesized and degraded until each copy would be pure craft and produced in a short time span. These paintings are called potboilers because they are mechanically and physically the same, and only serve for the artist to make a living. They are painted rapidly, in quick succession and in a planned, mechanical way, without the originality of the first painting. Some people get conflicted as to whether a potboiler is art or craft. As I have said, if there is no originality in subsequent paintings after the original, these paintings are potboilers and thus craft. There are many people who would argue this statement saying: "The colors may be different; the brush strokes are different; and the same artist is doing them." That's not enough to change them from being potboilers. Some would even argue the artist signed them. Many artists sign their prints, that doesn't change the print from being craft.

As we all know, when a craft exceeds all expectations it becomes art. When Andy Warhol took the craft of serigraphy (silkscreening) way beyond size expectations and color overlapping, those works became art. Jeff Koons envisioned metalworking could go to extremes, when he decided to make huge sculptures in polished stainless steel. It is art, no matter how banal it might seem to some viewers.

—————◆————

There are two examples of how a craft item becomes art as a result of time or alternate use: If a quantity of a craft item is made and time has reduced their number to a few or less, they may be considered art. And, if a craft item is brought into a work of art as part of an assemblage, it would be considered as being part of the work of art.

chapter ten

EXCLUSIVITY AND DIVISIVENESS

When observing universal truths, we have to consider all the influences affecting the art language we want to use: Sharp edges and points create tension, smooth rounded curves and feathered edges create a feeling of calm and serenity, light colors advance and dark colors recede, to name a few.

None of us are so free in our personal lives that we can accept everything. We draw a circle around ourselves defining where we won't go, or have outside influences enter. In this way we can accept and reconcile our own behavior.

The realities of life dictate personal preferences of like and dislike; we as artists have to deal with our creations more like scientists and unbiased reporters. We must separate the issue into its component parts by utilizing the Five Ws: Who are those who promote this issue? What condition and thinking are they trying to protect or promote? When did the issue come into our sphere? Where is the issue from, and why is it here? You can use the same process for anyone or anything, and you can ask many more questions. Also, it is not a good idea to have universal likes and dislikes at the same time unless it's part of the drama in your story.

Referring to human culture, we might say the definition is debatable at this time. For our purposes human culture means what we have done or the way we do things, such as artistic and intellectual achievements. There will always be someone who will challenge you, if you are not a part of a specific culture or you do not understand it. Culture is being used as a weapon as well as being used as a beacon to highlight wonderful achievements. Being aware of the meaning of your subject is important to get the right artistic representation.

Understanding the Freedom in Art means you have to be aware of the challenges to your beliefs, and you have to consider if your beliefs have real value. There is an ugly face on those who think they have the power to limit the freedoms within you because of some supposed ownership. We can respect thoughts and beliefs, on the other hand, we won't accept appropriated ownership of something in the public domain. Think of Japanese and African art principles and techniques freely applied by many European artists in the last part of the nineteenth and early twentieth centuries. This is an example of the Freedom in Art. African and Japanese cultures are still the same although modified by the passage of time. The belief that only certain people own certain behaviors or styles is absurd. Lines and colors don't change regardless of who uses them.

"When people demand exclusivity of anything in art, it creates a problem."

As knowledge and communication become more universal, the demand to document ones own history crops up loudly. There is an assumption that only a certain group should be allowed to document a select people because only they have the eyes and knowledge to recognize the emotional meaning.

There is a problem with people who perpetrate this kind of ownership: it is a violation of everything the Freedom in Art stands for. Are you not allowed to sing a song you heard on the radio? Do you own all the wild birds that roost on your property. This is the same kind of thinking. The appropriation these people attach causes the conflict created by their claim.

When people demand exclusivity of anything in art it creates division. Exclusivity only gives one side of a story, and may be corrupted in order to pursue an agenda which may or may not result in the truth. Also, those who are shut out may create images opposed to the advancement of the appropriated agenda. This leads to more division and confusion.

We have to respect the Freedom in Art, and the laws of our society. Many instances have occurred where people have appropriated something to further their own power and subject others to their will, whether it be legally or illegally. However, the Freedom in Art shows no regard for one appropriation or another from the public domain. Whether the case is a group of people appropriating a name or a word holding an emotional meaning as their own; or someone demanding exclusive rights to a certain style of art claiming the style in question has a cultural meaning and you would be stealing if you were to use it? Are we prepared to destroy all art of the past because we want to change history and have decided to rewrite it? Righting a wrong has many remedies that do not include breaking laws, universal truths or violating our rights. Claiming the Freedom in Art to create is your right; infringing on another person's rights is wrong when something is in the public domain.

If a creation is about, or includes general subjects such as religion, culture, race, ideology, politics, gender or sexual preferences, you have opened doors that cannot be judged on individual merit. Stereotyping is not used with these subjects. It is limited to use when the subject has an individual identity. Feelings should not be defined by how clever or knowledgeable a person is, and emotions should not be expressed as a puzzle leading others to try to discover a meaning. The worth of anything individual should not be depicted as universal. Therefore, you are better off sticking to a definite "yes or no" subject, character or individual.

chapter eleven

THE UNDISCIPLINED SUBJECTS OF POLITICS, IDEOLOGY, RELIGION, RACE AND NATIONALITY

Politics

Now and again we work with subjects that are more difficult. We, as artists, dislike following outside influences; because we are free to render whatever we want objectively and on an individual basis, and we allow the viewer to offer up their own interpretation. It is important to have the utmost respect for every viewer of art, regardless of what biases they may have. Also, for every artist to understand they have total control over their art, this creates a partnership with the viewer. And finally, we have to recognize the humble nature of the artist, and know they cannot be all things to all people.

"Sometimes artists have the urge to solve a problem through their art."

Solving political problems through your creativity changes the Freedom in Art concept because you become subjective, and you're impressing a personal influence on the story. Being totally free in your art has to mean you're totally objective. Conflicts occur within us all the time, and it's your decision how much objective influence you want to use. No matter how strongly you want to show your subjective face in a work of art, you must remain impartial. Sometimes you'll find being neutral is also your subjective self. When you decide to follow a certain political agenda, you have taken art without an agenda and divided it into numerous factions pitting against one another, forgetting the equal competition in the open arena.

Let's gather the facts for a story about politics:

Several people, young and old, are at a poling station and we observe the involvement of money, influence, greed, power and those who receive or abuse it. Suppose we now have the bare facts and we must decide what to do. It's all about being creative. First, we know politics is serious business, because it involves everything in our lives in one respect or another. The only equalizer to make it human is humor, and our ability to find mistakes or flaws, and sometimes be able to criticize. We now have the makings of a story, turning a subjective into an objective using humor.

Here's the story:

People are gathered at a poling station ready to vote. There's an adult holding a slogan banner amongst the group. The slogan banner reads, "VOTE JOE CABBAGE, HE'LL GIVE YOU MONEY!" The holder of the banner is bending over and giving a lollipop to a child. He has money hanging out of his back pocket and adults are smiling and ready to pluck the money. Another sign says, "VOTE HERE TODAY." Do these facts tell the story and make you smile? We immediately know who's voting, the banner holder is buying votes from willing adults and trying to influence a young child (a future voter) by giving the child candy. Is the scene ironic? The mental picture is a universal theme, telling the story without further explanation and embodies many humorous perceptions people have.

Even with care to be very objective, there will inevitably be someone who will find fault in a rendition even if it is done in jest; or because it was done in jest.

Ideology

On occasion you have to take a step back and look at the big picture which is often difficult. You first have to gather the facts. If you don't know much about the subject, grab a dictionary or go online to research it. In this case, we'll use the Oxford Dictionary definition of ideology: The manner of thinking characteristic of a class of people, or an individual. Because ideology is an outer influence, we have lots of leeway in using it as a subject which opens up a vast array of styles we can choose from to tell the story as a work of art. Determine the parameters of the ideology, such as: Who practices the specific way of thinking and what do they want from you, me, and society? Are they more religious? Do the believers not want to be part of the society they live in? What do they promote or espouse? Are they practicing their beliefs now? Where do they practice it? Is there a compelling reason why people believe in this ideology? We'll put together two stories with differing plots.

In the first example:

We have a group of people who are an open society believing in the inner strength of the soul; they have taken an oath to live with nature, promoting peace and goodwill for all living things. For this group, it is the pathway to heaven.

In this story, you have a peaceful group of participants who want and promote the best in conjunction with Mother Nature; they believe the good they do is the stairway to heaven. With the use of flowing lines and tinted neutral colors, this ideology can be told within a small area.

In a second example:

A group of angry young men have formed a secret society at their college. Their desire is to promote the peaceful overthrow of government by the use of computers and subliminal messages on the internet, supporting the return of a lawful government.

In this narration, a group of angry young men use their cunning to overthrow a corrupt institution so they may have a law-abiding government and a peaceful society. The story requires jagged lines to show anger and brash, bold colors, which recede to neutrals. This shows the intent to positively impact society. A large canvas should be used to show the universal nature of the ideology.

Two different stories, with compelling reasons to exist. Both of these stories can be approached in the same way, through the mind using the building blocks of art: points, lines, planes, a symbolic approach, and color. Add technique, and you've done it.

"Musicians can hear the sound of a musical instrument being played in their mind."

In reading, it is possible to picture what is said through the mind's eye. All styles of art can tell a story; the most complete being representational art, and the least being abstract art. Nevertheless, the artist and the viewer work together in a large degree to relate the story. When you're putting together a storyline, think in terms of painting with your mind so you can feel the tension, the drama, and the resolve or conclusion of the narrative. The process works for the visual artist, seeing all the parts and movements to be used to create a work of art. Visualizing your goal in your mind's eye is something you must learn how to do.

I chose to make both of these ideology paintings abstract works of art so the artist statement would be stronger. And, you must add an individual stamp on them so they won't be viewed as propaganda.

Religion

Humans are imprinted with everything the senses absorb from the time they are babies. The stories of peoples' lives are filled with principles and for many, their belief in religion. We can't ignore the fact that outer beliefs can, and do, affect who you are in the physical sense. Religion is not grounded in reality because it takes faith to be a believer. Nevertheless, religion has great sway in the lives of many.

"The appeal of art transcends all barriers."

We, as humans, admire the nature of art because it can exceed our expectations. The problems arise when people decide they like the power of art, and then attempt to control it for their own purposes, often to manipulate others. In the present tense art is universal, and should not be limited in any way by subjective influences.

Up to this day, art has often been used to advance the narrative of religion. It has also been censored in one way or another by different factions of society to control and direct the human condition. Often, these practices limit the instilled freedoms in art.

The metaphysical nature of a mountain is still a mountain even if you build radio towers on top of it. Only the soul of the mountain as nature created it is tarnished.

Another facet of art is the inherent freedom that it can destroy itself in the name of art. Art is in the eyes of the beholder, because it mirrors us in all ways, that is why it's so feared and revered.

Let's create a work of art about religion:
We'll approach the subject from a diverse angle. Say we don't use the colors purple and carmine (long thought to be divine colors), and instead make a statement in mostly green, with some yellow, and a touch of blue, keeping a balance of light and dark. Let's turn the field of

action (the vertical rectangular canvas) to the right some degrees. Now, we have consciously directed our narrative in ways that make it more difficult for us to create a story. We have challenged ourselves to create something more dynamic than what we could otherwise do.

Let's put our story together with the facts we have. You might be thinking we don't have any facts yet; but we do, in colors and shapes and we'll fit them together to build our story. We're going to use mostly green, and plants are mostly green; apply some yellow, and sunshine is yellow; a bit of blue, and the sky is blue. We have skewed the field of action to the right, so our story will read from left to right. Our hero is the color green, and that color is fighting to reach the light of yellow, past the emptiness of blue and the symbolic use of light and dark lines. The action is intense and the speed has accelerated with the leaning canvas.

This story is based on facts, told in a non-traditional way. Earth, as created, demands all things on the planet must be fed to grow, and fulfill their purpose in the scheme of life. It's not an easy existence, and everything living must fight for its own space and sustenance to procreate. What a story! We were able to tell it in a universal language all people have the capacity to understand by using color, lines and asymmetry.

Race

Another subject some people think is protected and off-limits to outsiders is race. The principles of the Freedom in Art maintain there's no subject that cannot be fairly addressed including those under intense scrutiny, protectionism, power-of-will, or corruption. Then again, you have to decide for yourself how important the subject is.

The swastika is a good example of a symbol representing a people, their race and ideology chosen for use by the Nazi Party of Germany during the early to middle years of the twentieth century. The figure originated 6,000 years ago and was called the swastika meaning well-being in the Sanskrit language of ancient India. The Nazi connected strong cultural, racial and ideological sentiments to the symbol. That attachment proved to be so strong, the symbol, only lines put together in a specific way, will have a negative meaning for centuries. The tyranny these lines represent in memories of atrocities, tremendous fear and hatred, live in the minds of millions of people.

The symbol has also been used by several Native American cultures of the Southwest United States and can simply be a native design from anywhere in the world. It is a decorative form and sometimes used as a symbol representing an idea. In native culture it has been known as the "Whirling Log." Many designs originate from their use in crafts with a warp and weft, like in the weaving of baskets and blankets.

You can see how art can be used freely, and it can also be appropriated from artists and removed from the encyclopedia of tools available because of its use. Being obstructive in our thinking may often divide us into groups and sub-groups, build walls between us, claim ownership of thoughts, movements and universal truths.

There are legal means to protect intellectual property. Those premises don't prevent the thinking that ownership is exclusive because someone says so and is willing to intimidate others.

Inner and outer forces can create negative thoughts that will dominate our minds at some time in our lives. It is not that those thoughts have lived in us, but recognizing the problems and then ridding ourselves of their influence, make all of us better artists.

Nationality

Creating art is easier when the subject is isolated from an artists' inner influences and thinking. The identity of a people can be difficult because it can be very personal. Most of the time, nationality is a subject that is treated in a lighthearted tone with some humor. Characters are numerous in the subject: the Scotsman who's hardly understood due to the heavy brogue in his voice; the Englishman, formal with a stiff upper lip; the Russian with a bottle of vodka in one hand, and a Kalashnikov rifle slung over a shoulder; the Italian gigolo or mafia figure, and an American wearing a cowboy hat. There are stereotypes for every group of people on earth and you can see how easily those characterizations can be used. During times of conflict, opposing sides use negative stereotypes to demonize one another.

"Having pride in who and what you are makes you a better person."

In this day and age, there are many outside influences seeking to refute the historical characterization of some nationalities and people because of the unequal distribution of knowledge and technology. Of course, those people who had a written language first had the knowledge and ability to document their times ahead of the rest, and thus were followed by other groups to carry on the same work for posterity. Those people who did not find it necessary to document their existence, have been the last people to adopt a common language to create a historical record. They are the ones who are most likely to refute the historical record written and characterized by people outside their group. The desire of self-characterization has become very strong and evident in the art world. The idea that we can change history and judge the people of the past by our current standards is unreasonable.

There are trends in the world view of people, wiping out many thousands of general, and individual identities through commercialization.

Clothing has moved to universal styles in almost every area on earth. A hundred years ago, clothing and adornment, were a way to identify a people and where they were from. Today, western style clothing appears to be universal in industrial countries and is making inroads in non-industrial nations wiping out cultural ways of dressing and adornment. Many countries encourage traditional dress and music on national holidays to retain their culture.

In this chapter, we have addressed five of the most volatile subjects. Each can be explosive in the minds of many people. By limiting each subject to individuals demanding a "yes or no" answer; the subject is neutralized and separated from being expressed as an influence to being viewed objectively. It's not surprising that human beings want to be accepted as individuals.

chapter twelve

THE KILLER INSTINCT

If you're confused about the meaning of one of your paintings, you won't be alone, the viewer will be confused as well. You will never be able to assign a balanced story to the painting and everybody will know it, but they won't use the same words you just read or have a kind sentiment for your work.

We have to have the killer instinct to survive in the world of art, and that means we always have to put our best foot forward. Does this mean you have to be mean and aggressive toward other artists in the competition of the open arena? No, it doesn't. Does it mean you have to be publicly abusive toward anyone who disagrees with your philosophy. No, it does not. Well, you might ask, what does it mean? You have to be strong enough to destroy work you know has problems, and which, you should not be willing to present to the open arena in its current circumstance and condition. Because, those paintings are not up to the standards you have set for yourself; meaning you have to kill many creations you have invented or will invent.

We all have possessive feelings about every work we create. Most artists who have strong feelings about their creations and agonize over them, are not thinking about the consequences of what they are doing. Exposing your beliefs or your soul is not creative, in most cases, it is downright boring. Nobody wants to hear or see your problems, they have problems of their own they are trying to work out. That's why they go to art venues, to relax. We have to take control of those feelings and use our judgment to realize a painting with flaws is many times harder to correct in time and brain power than it is to destroy, or otherwise rub out and start all over again.

"Only mental health professionals care about the influences of who and what you are in your art."

This is where you have to use your mind's eye to "see" all your moves and expected results in your next project before you put paint to canvas. This means no "seat-of-the-pants" painting.

If you believe Vincent van Gogh put all his feelings into his paintings, think again. He had an outstanding technique that nobody else used which made his paintings different. His personal feelings and emotions were set aside when he painted; he was the consummate painter in his compartment. The powerful stories about his torment, rage and self-hatred were brought forth after he died. What they left out of the vision of what they wrote, was the tremendous determination he had to create and whose art was before its time of acceptance. Look at the paintings of the last year of his life and you will see none of the psychological torment that has been said about him.

If something doesn't work out, it doesn't mean you're a failure. It just means it didn't work out. You will grow by finding out what went wrong and not repeating those mistakes.

Many artists want to dive in and start a project "seat-of-the-pants," that's a big mistake. If you do this, you are subconsciously assuming you already have the answers to every problem.

The answer is to plan your production from one step to the next. Imagine yourself building a house and thinking of many moves in advance. The process gets easier in time. The payoff is: you get stronger and more confident in your art. And, your production is safe as long as you know the plan and how you are going to get to your goal.

There are those who have thought about problems in the act of creating; sometimes for hours, and other times for days, until they come up with an answer they are happy with. These situations usually take place when an artist is creating "seat-of-the-pants," beginning with a goal, not ending with it. A better plan is to work through your story in your mind's eye and correct problems before they arise than to start with an idea that has no plan. Not knowing what your goal is makes it difficult to get to a conclusion.

Writing the steps you will take to achieve your goal is a good way to keep your mind clear and not get boxed in while waiting for the canvas to tell you what to do next. Often, when you are in production without a plan, you expend so much energy thinking about solutions you end up hating your creation. It is wise to let the work sit out of sight until you feel you can face it again with a fresh outlook, or, wipe the canvas clean and start over again with a proper plan. In these situations, the adage "familiarity breeds contempt" gets directly in your face. The truth is: the more you have on your mind in the form of doubt and uncertainty, the longer it will take you to complete your production. Ease your mind and consider writing while you are under pressure and you have a lot of ideas floating around. Divide the structure of your project into the Five Ws to expound on each in turn. Identify the subject you want to be the focus of the production and then question why. Continue asking the question to each of the Ws until you are convinced you have all the answers you need, and then begin, or continue the production, because you now have a plan.

Universal truths are diminished when we abstract a story. Nevertheless, with the knowledge of the Freedom in Art, you are allowed to do whatever you want; you are the one who puts the parameters in place to target the audience you want. If you don't like an example, change it. Don't accept one idea as the absolute end of the story; you are the final arbiter. Think of something representational. Write several stories with different techniques, and select the one you think is the most unique and will have the greatest impact on the viewer. Coming up with a story and how to apply it in a creation is probably the easiest step in your production schedule. You can change styles, colors and techniques within seconds, without putting anything on canvas.

If you want to practice the generic beat sheet (the Five Ws) of the principles of the Freedom in Art, apply it to your daily life. Going to the grocery store, taking a vacation or planning a day at home, any one of these ideas will work. Write down everything you do. Then, when you get to the climax of the day write down the goals you have reached and work backward to piece your story together with drama and conflict, because now you know the end of the story. When you are doing this exercise, the first thing you will notice is that you are doing it "seat-of-the-pants." That's right, the mind is conditioned to doing everything "seat-of-the-pants," because, in reality, we cannot jump ahead in time to know the end result until time has advanced and reality has set in. The key to doing this is planning to do it every day and then getting it done until you get comfortable with the process of writing a story.

> *In a story, everything starts at the end and the beginning is created or becomes an altered reality. If you say, "I want to see the northern lights from inside the Arctic Circle!", that's the end of the story. Everything leading up to that moment is the rest of the story. And, getting motivated to take the first step of preparation is the beginning.*

Not all paintings created by successful artists of the past demand top dollar; why? There is no secret here, compare paintings by any of those successful artists and use your knowledge to ask critical questions, and you will be able to easily see why one painting is worth much more than another. The success of one painting and its promotional abilities does not necessarily carry over to other works of art by the same artist, it can only bring notice to other works, be they the same quality or not.

There are some marketing reasons why a small painting may fit into a low price range to attract a specific demographic of buyer; and a large, complex painting is purposely in a higher price range. However, the quality should remain the same. Often early and experimental works don't demand the attention and price points as later productions. This is where you have to use your judgment and realize all these artists attempted to keep a high level of quality in every work they sent to the open arena at a certain point in time. Keep in mind that the beholder has the most control over what will succeed.

One reason many artists don't have success in their early years is because they have not organized their art process or established a solid foundation. They analyze their every thought and motion until they are brain dead. Those movements create walls for them to get over and the longer they spend thinking about their problems, the higher the walls become and they give up on their dreams. That's why you have to have the killer instinct, to overcome all those bad habits and directly address the problems posed by your production. Get rid of your walls of obstruction, and move on as quickly as possible.

Here's a challenge: Write down the issues you have about art. Then, put the paper out of sight; knowing those problems are not forgotten. Now, get back to working on your next project. In five or six weeks, look at your list. You probably won't recognize much of what you wrote as problems because most of them were a figment of your imagination.

As you write stories using the facts of the Five Ws, some people get tired of what they think is the sameness of what they're doing. This feeling doesn't occur to everybody; for those of you who find your-selves faced with this situation, look to a new subject, and ask difficult questions so the need to surpass into something new is resolved without falling off a cliff. Don't forget, you have to have the killer instinct in the back of your mind at all times as you work. If you only exercise this option when you bull your way into a brain jam, you have already made the major mistake of not preparing yourself and your production properly. It is better to throw away dozens of ideas than to agonize over one. In this situation, you can also fall back on the standby option of painting something that is the "same but different," because you are still painting and getting experience.

It is human nature to make the simple into something complex, and to seek understanding for an ambiguous issue having no resolution. As an artist you'll learn to love and hate the outside world because you're opening up to allow objective understanding of all points of view. Your imagination won't be clouded by the reality of the world we live in. Finding a new place to live in your dreams is often a godsend that every artist wishes they had transcended into permanently. The reality is that we do not live our everyday lives in our dreams, and we can control what we do. The exercise of practicing this type of transformation changes your perception of who you are, and presents doors that have never been open to you. The greatest difficulty is breaking out of your comfortable mental environment and stepping into a larger one, giving you a deeper understanding of the world and of those around you.

<hr />

"Gamble your way to a new future on purpose."

Here is another option when you are having a hard time thinking of what to create. We don't want you to give up on your desires in art due to stumbling over the story issue. There's no magic in the answer to the problem. Most artists have faced this situation, and many have a difficult time whenever they decide to begin a new project. The unknown and how you make it simple is challenging, but it can be done with chance as the mediator. Even those of you who feel very confident in your ability to create a story from any given subject should begin to create tools so you'll have them at your disposal.

Get five bowls and label each with one of the Five Ws. Write on small pieces of card stock ten examples for each of the Ws and put them in their respective bowls. When you are ready, draw one card from each bowl and you have the beginning of your next story. You now have a diverse and random way you can come up with stories that will keep you forever busy if you so desire to use this solution. As you think of new examples, add them to the bowls. You can reject this idea if you want; however, the next time you are stumped for an answer to begin a project, use this procedure and I'll guess you will be very pleased with what you come up with. If you are in the dumps over the project you have drawn first, put the cards back in the bowls, mix them up, and draw again; do this until you find something that will fit your mood.

⋙◆⋘

The killer instinct serves a major purpose other than quality. Your process of creating is to go from one production to another quickly and without hesitation or mental torment. Knowing you are making a product you will be proud of because you know how and why it is created.

There is no denying this process frees up the mind and allows the artist to produce a tremendous amount of work that costs money. This issue does have an impact on every artist. Few artists can afford to have a large studio and storage space. You have to cut your expenses and the amount of space needed to store your creations by reducing the use of expensive materials and using supports that don't take up much room. It's more important to produce a lot of high quality inexpensive art than it is to produce a lesser number of costly art that takes up a lot of storage space.

chapter thirteen

SEX, NUDES AND LOVE

These three topics are bundled together because each exists with one or more of the others. The history of art has been littered with sex, nudes and love from the beginning. Both positive and negative images and descriptions have been repeated over and over again.

Of all the subjects you can think of, sex is the most universally understood (and misunderstood) of any because of its physical nature. Do you think creating a work of art on the subject of sex is easy? It's actually one of the toughest subjects. It doesn't matter what you create; your audience will be limited to those who see something other than what is depicted.

Nudes are universally judged like they were in a beauty contest, and the viewer is looking for perfection. Technique is a crucial component along with the Five Ws. The eye is very precise to put order in the human figure, especially when the figures are portrayed without clothing. One reason you see over-exaggeration, cartoon figures, and comedy instilled in these works of art is to overcome all the outer influences in the viewer to gain greater acceptance.

There are thousands of questions on the subject of love and its emotional nature. For the artist, there is only one question to ask: "What does love mean?"

Let's try a few stories:

Love is when you help your child get dressed before sending them off to school in the morning. This is more than enough information to come up with an interesting work of art.

Let's say a mom is helping her son get ready to go to school by zipping his coat up while he drinks orange juice and holds onto his soccer ball and lunch bag. Known and assumed answers to the Five Ws are all there, and it will be easy to paint a story realistically.

Next:

Love is a dad rooting for his son's football team. Yes, we have most of the Five Ws, so here is another easy story to paint. Let's paint this story on two canvases in cartoon style. In the first canvas we see a boy running with a football under his arm and waving to his dad, who is jumping up and down on the sideline. In the second canvas we see the beginning of a dog pile, and the boy loses his grip on the ball. His dad is still rooting for him, even though the scoreboard shows his son's team is losing. You could paint these canvases as if they were playing the game at night under stadium lights, giving a great contrast to the characters against a dark background.

Finally:

Love displays passion by giving a houseplant a trim on a sunny day. You have to assume the plant needs a trim. Let's do something really different now; we're going to make it an abstract. The movements of lines and colors have to symbolically show the action of trimming the houseplant, and your perspective has to allow room for the Five Ws. Use your imagination on this one and see it in your mind's eye. Bold, bright colors would be great.

chapter fourteen

PASSION

A subject has to have something to make it sing and grab a viewers' sensibilities. Passion is what the spirit within you gives to a work of art. It can also be a story in its own right.

The Freedom in Art gives you the opportunity to have a series in your line of creations, because every work has a different plot. You can have a different story, different characters, different colors, and keep your style of painting the same to knit your series together. You can mix and match as you want. Many of the Abstract Expressionists had wonderful stories; the paintings they created supported what they were thinking, and that passionate thinking lifts the art to another level.

You have a choice: do you prefer to hear a viewer say, "I love the color red in that painting!" about one of your abstracts? Or, would you rather hear a viewer say, "That red color builds a scream in me when I see the way it floats across the sky!" The first example is bland and without a foundation, and the latter has a passionate story that can be read even though it's an abstract.

"A series of your art is like a novel broken up into chapters."

Imagination plays an incredible role in the minds of creators and viewers, and these roles in turn work together. Most people rely on imprinted knowledge, and look for the obvious imprint first, like the human face. You can see examples in everyday advertising. People also love to look at clouds and mountains to see things from their imprinted knowledge. Maybe they see a bunny rabbit or the face of an old man in the clouds. By exercising the freedom you have in your imagination, your stories will be built upon a stronger foundation. Allow your mind to go where it has never gone before by asking random questions. Then, ask practical questions that work. Like, how can that be possible? Or, how can it fit into my story? Look at it in terms of abstract ideas.

When I was a boy of ten or so, I used to lay in bed looking at the ceiling of the room I shared with my brother. It had a plaster ceiling and there were unorganized trowel marks over the entire area. I used my imagination to see and find figures in the trowel marks and the shadows made by them. My mother enjoyed listening to me when I would tell her about what I discovered.

Let's write a story about passion:

Being passionate is when you hug someone while you watch the sunset. That's enough information to find the Five Ws. We're going to replace figures with colors and lines. Let's pick dark blue for a "who" man, a dark rose for a "who" woman; these two colors are sinuously together, joined with a "what" line. The color light orange will represent the "when" sunset, and lines will represent the "where" outdoors. All the color and lines have to be sinuous, representing passion. The Five Ws will be knit together with transparent yellow green for the "why." The composition isn't complicated; there's no difference in using symbols in painting as using different words in writing. In your mind, think about the possibilities and the technique you want to use; there's a great deal of wiggle room here. You do need to do more thinking and be more creative in the situations you want to portray, and that shouldn't be too hard.

"Arouse passion in what you see, without it, the world would indeed be a dull place."

chapter fifteen

SITUATIONS

Now, we're getting back to more fun stuff to work with. Not to say the subjects we've been working with are not fun; they are more challenging and have many more influences, and, they ring a different note.

Situational subjects cover the gamut of thought in any direction you want to go. They are things that happen in daily life which create artistic contrast of one measure or another, and those circumstances are what make life interesting. None of us are perfect and we're not mind readers, so situations are plentiful. The first example I encountered when I was a boy of two or three, was when I went to the grocery store with my mother. I was overwhelmed with the aroma of fruit and vegetables and things to see; I pulled on my mother's coat to ask her a question and a lady turned around and asked, "What do YOU want?" She wasn't my mother. I was scared to death! My mother came from behind and grabbed me, saying I should stay right with her, or I might get lost. My mother and the lady laughed together over the situation. They were both wearing the same style and color of coat.

Thinking about my situation, you can see all the Five Ws. There are numerous pictures we can create. We could even look at this story as a great opportunity to make it an abstract painting. Converting a story from representational into abstract is a good way to keep in the practice of looking for something different and unusual. It's wonderful to be an adventurer, and to go places you haven't gone before to discover something new.

Let's create a collage:

Paint different colors on card stock, then use heavy shears to cut these cards into various shapes. Use many colors and a lot of cards, then select a hard base to glue the card stock onto. Draw the figures of your story on the board. Position the different cards as you would if you were painting using blocks of color. Start with the larger blocks first, that way if you don't like the first cutouts you have enough uncut space to cut smaller areas from them. If you see something interesting, photograph it so you'll have a record and continue to change your cards at will. This will allow you to discover new shapes and configurations. Sometimes you have to go through many different set-ups before you feel you have enough to have your photos printed. Often, printing these on paper in black and white is a good way to see contrasts and where they will be in your composition. Another option is downloading the pictures to your computer; put them into a photo program and arrange them like you want. Later, test other ways to arrive at the same result. After you have an acceptable arrangement, photo and then print it out in color. You'll then use the photo to arrange the cards back on the board and glue them down to complete the finished artwork. By using technique to finish the creation, you've compiled your story in abstract terms.

This is fun stuff which begs you to write a moral to the story, but finding the moral is sometimes more difficult.

**"Use your imagination by going places you have
never been before or getting lost in a city knowing you are
not in danger, because you have the knowledge to
find your way back to normal."**

chapter sixteen

MORALS AND ETHICS

It's easy to write a story when the meaning of your subject is clearly defined. When you have a subject whose meaning is ambiguous, it is much more difficult. Then, you have to use your ability to make credible decisions and often to make judgment calls. Use your artist privilege to include or exclude what is moral or ethical. You will have to think about your target audience, which is an outer influence in itself.

*If you have to consider what is mainstream or what you want to **make** moral or ethical, strike it from your work. Because, this would be your subjective self putting an influence on your project and it would no longer be objective, it would be propaganda. Remember, because the law says one thing, does not mean your audience feels the same way. The law isn't an artist, you are.*

Recently, there was an article in the news about a young college student being arrested for urinating next to the front door of a nightclub featuring a punk rock band. The bouncer was an off-duty police officer, and had the young man arrested on a moral turpitude charge and lewd conduct in public. This is a great example of a story with the Five Ws. There's nothing ambiguous about the story. Does this story disgust you to the point where you wouldn't want to talk about it? You should be open enough to read and discuss anything but you don't have to act upon the information. Story ideas come from a multiple of directions, and they are all part of your resource library.

"Morally correct art is neither good or bad; you have to rate it by audience reaction."

It doesn't matter what you say or do in art today, we are faced with the fact that it will be qualified by hints and tags from outside the world of art. You must stick to the story attached to your art and back it up with absolute conviction. Often, you can find a good story for a painting by paying attention to the events happening in your area. You don't have to make up a story; it's all there in the news. By being open-minded and having a desire to chronicle the human condition, articles in the news or social media are a great asset, and much of the work is already done for you. You do have to be cautious about the bent of a story, especially if it's political. You can see how stories get easier to find if you know where to look and what to watch out for. Being a reporter of the human condition, as well as a story teller and a producer, you can ask all the "what if" questions you want, which makes you much more than a reporter. You are a person who is creative and wants to know the whole story. But, do not confuse what you do as the only truth, because there's always more to be known behind the scenes.

The subject of morals and ethics are next to each other because they are married. Morals are the main subject, and ethics are the principles and ideals of morals in society. Maybe ethics should be called the conscience of morals. Perhaps you can pick and choose from the meaning of these two words.

For our purposes, view ethics as the balance wheel between the good and the bad because they are in the eyes of the beholder. The more bad there is in a subject, the more you need to balance it with good. This is what makes a great story like David against Goliath, the oppressed against the machine, and the righteous against the depraved. Any of the subjects we have talked about, and will talk about, are enhanced by your judgment to add a measure of morals or ethics.

chapter seventeen

JUDGMENT

What you think, is very important in what you do; and what you have done is made a judgment call. This means you have made a decision to act upon your opinion on what is the best course of action out of many. When someone else is judging you by their standards (most of the time unbeknownst to you) they are giving you a personal view that may ignore and not coincide with your own judgment.

We would not have art as you see it today if the judges from academia and the Salon in Paris had their way in the nineteenth century, exercising their values on what was good art. This concern for who and why their work was judged is the reason the Impressionists believed in "no judges and no juries."

A creator of a work of art is the only one who may make judgments on their creations. The viewer only has the right to like it or not and a critic of art may judge art in accordance with their criteria. This is a subtle distinction but it is important to show you the difference. It's advisable to listen to what critics say because many have up-to-date thoughts, but, review those reflections with caution.

The most out of the way comment any viewer can make to an artist is to liken their creation to the work of another artist. When a statement like this is made out of the viewer's like or dislike context it changes the meaning of the art being viewed. This is the viewers' way of stereotyping a vision and it demeans the story the artist is trying to put forth. Often, the viewer is not aware of the meaning of what they say because they are not knowledgeable in the language of art. I do believe there are many artists who feel honored when their art is likened to that of another, especially if they hold the other artist in their esteem. However, they are missing the point of the negative comment.

> *An inventor can use any technique available at their discretion but certainly does not own it. For someone to say the Tesla automobile has tires just like the Ford Model A borders on the ridiculous. This is simply expounding on the obvious.*

Although there are many artists who base their careers on their ability to paint like others, there's no doubt that even if you've never seen the work of other artists, you'll be using techniques and styles they are using or have used. The judgment as to what techniques you use should not be questioned. None-the-less, it is bad form to liken an artist's work to that of another.

"Be yourself, because nobody really thinks you're someone else."

Even if an artist can leap-frog into the future without having years of experience, it is a good policy to study the history of what has been accomplished, what you like, and to keep abreast of what contemporary creators are doing. It is also important to place an identity on your creations so you can separate them from all the rest.

> *If you line up ten artists and each in turn have to talk about their creations; who do you think will receive the most attention when you identify your subject and clearly tell the story of your work with all the drama, laughter, and tension it deserves?*

chapter eighteen

APPRECIATE ART

Nothing speaks more loudly at an art exhibit than the words "I like it," followed by a smile on the face of the speaker. These words don't say the art is good or exceptional; they say the viewer has made a link with the art and is willing to give it the chance it deserves. Those words are music to an artist's ears and they're the door that opens the connection between the artist and the viewer.

Art becomes very personal when you are willing to bring it into your home because you like it.

After any introduction to a work of art, a viewer looks for beauty to sustain their decisions. The essence of Impressionism is the lasting beauty the style has, which overcomes time and the dreaded words "old art."

"ART is your mosaic of LIFE."

Every artist has a fondness for certain styles of painting; this means an artist can also be a part of the audience of another artist. This is art you cherish to look at and have a wonderful emotional connection with. Chances are a certain style of art has had a strong influence on you and may have been the catalyst to sway you towards the work you do.

It is necessary to recognize influences so you can put them aside when you're in the compartment. The reason for this special isolation is to be in your personal compartment alone, and without influences. This might lead you to create something totally new instead of trying to create something you enjoy unless you are using the "same but different" principle.

Those thoughts bring up a question: Why would you want to create something you don't like? Your rejection of this thought might find you to be someone who wishes to recreate the wheel again and stay in your own comfort zone. Or, the answer could lead you to be a person who's trying to further art by taking it into new territories. This might be the test for you to realize exactly what kind of person you are. Many of the most revered artists have become famous not because their art was pretty but because they took art into new territory. Sometimes, that meant they didn't have to like what they produced, but they took art into the realm of the unseen and different.

"Appreciating your art is better than liking it."

The art world is a balance between like and dislike and has moved beyond artists creating only what they like. You have to challenge yourself to create outside the box by thinking before you create. Many artists disdain moving out of their comfort zones and paint in the same style throughout their careers. Some find their art crossing over into other styles of painting unintentionally, and yet, others purposefully step out of their style and paint in another style because they want to stretch their abilities to gain a new audience or to keep up with the changing tastes of their current audience. You do have to be more sophisticated in your ideas to create a work that seems to go beyond your level of being. Make sure not to go in circles.

Remember, sometimes it is good to paint a work "just because" so you can keep yourself landed; and, these paintings are "keepers" for you and your family.

chapter nineteen

OVERCOMING DISLIKES

All our senses look for perfection, beauty, and personal preference. This focus on beauty is why much of what we call new is at first glance considered disdainful. As we accept the ugly we diminish what we consider ideal. Not every work of art has the universal nature that allows every viewer to be touched in the same way. In fact, pssst, there has never been such a universal work of art.

Due to the unequal nature of humanity, civilization has endeavored to adjust equality on a social level. Unfortunately, the art world has to accommodate so many levels of humanity, it is impossible to adjust everything equally without damaging the facts, eliminating competition and altering freedoms.

The person who is unable to compete in a bathing suit competition may be a blockbuster winner in a singing contest or a mathematical test. At sometime in our lives each person makes sense of where their talents lie and concentrates their efforts to nurture that ability, including altering other aspects of their assets to support their true calling like a singer/dancer who becomes a popular dramatic actor. Sometimes, we are born with natural assets which we have no original work or control over but must maintain, and other times we must learn and practice an endeavor to stand out in a given field.

"Competition in the open arena is the great equalizer."

There is an implication in the examples you have just read which affect all of us, and that is the demand for the elimination of the open arena and an open competition. Life is a challenge and each and every one of us is capable of excelling at something. Without the open arena we are left with an agenda to judge art.

Albert Einstein was not the best student when he went to school. If top grades were the qualifier for success, he may have never been recognized as one of the greatest minds in the history of humanity had he not submitted to the open arena to be recognized for the work he did. Also, in professional sports there's always one group of athletes who will dominate. Because, each one of those athletes went to the open arena and were the best the sport was looking for.

"Would it be a good idea to have professional basketball for players under five feet tall?"

There are special aptitudes that have to be developed to be an artist: you have to have vision; you have to be an adventurer; and you have to be a thinker who is self-motivated. You also have to be able to work out problems that will arise in the movements of your vision to get to a goal, and have the desire to be innovative in this pursuit. All this is above and beyond your physical and mental skills to actually create a work of art. Thus, each attempt on the part of a creator is a stepping stone going to infinity because none of us know where the final footprint will land.

For the artist, there will be numerous stop signs in a career, and you will see offers for other routes to follow. You might be tempted by something new that excites and compels you to try a new direction without changing your career architecture. Consider, the first time you veer from the avenue to your career goal, you've lost confidence in your plan, and most of the trust you have built up. You are in total control and at the top of your game when you have your career plan in place and ready to go from beginning to end. Leave those new thoughts for when you decide you are forced to make an adjustment in the architecture to your life goal. Write them down and describe the conditions that make them important in your architecture, which you will have to do at sometime in your future as you grow and develop. Some artists are capable of having a career on the fast track and changing their career path often, but they are rare.

—⊷⊶—

There's a natural lack of confidence in the mind of viewers, because they've been bombarded with an innumerable number of explanations that sound very reasonable for them to like or dislike a work of art. There are two options for the artist: accept reasonable doubt in the eyes of the beholder that allows the viewer to take control, or defend your creation with a strong story. Do not think you're overcoming objections; viewers rarely have objections which are judgmental in nature, they can simply like or dislike what they're looking at. Every viewer has attached qualities and values which the artist has no control over. You're never going to know their mind and experience, so you have to take the path you know best, and not waver. Respect the fact that not everyone will like your art, that's the freedom the viewer owns.

If someone unknown to you responds to your creation with suggestions or criticism, that behavior changes their status from being a viewer. They then become critics in some disguise, and you as an artist do not have to respect that status when your creations are involved. If they are speaking of the work of another artist, respect may be given to their observations. You can say the former statement would be subjective and the latter objective.

chapter twenty

OBSTACLES TO GET OVER

L et's speak further about your place and the roll of others. This is the status that stands between you as an artist, and the viewer: You are equal to one another in all respects regardless of inner or outer influences. The artist does not own the feelings and emotions within a creation. The viewer does not own a talent further than like or dislike. From the artist's point of view, they can only answer to what they control. We cannot control what others think or do. I say: "Be informed, be cautious, and be on the right side." The status of the artist and viewer must never be demeaned.

—◆—

There seems to be a universal feeling that the artist is the one who is at the convenience of everybody else for a multitude of reasons. Most notably, that the artist is the seller and the other person is the buyer.

We've talked a lot about what it is to be an artist, a creator, and an inventor, and only touched on the other side of the coin, the people who promote art.

Some individuals have the belief artists are a dime a dozen. They may be right about one thing, there are millions of practicing artists in the world at any given time. What they are wrong about is the belief artists are of no value.

"The spirit in art is not the same as the business of art, although, the business of art doesn't exist without the spirit in art."

There is an arrogance attached to the belief all artists are like pavement on the ground, and you have to be magnanimous when you begin to understand and deal with those issues. Whether you are submitting a proposal to exhibit or seeking representation, you have to work around what you might see as inherent faults with diplomacy. What you are seeking from museum curators or gallerists is a "yes or no" answer. Being selected is more a matter of chance than it is about art. Not being accepted or chosen is not the measure of the quality of your work. If you get a "yes," you are accepting a job to do. If you get a "no," you must be grateful for the other side to have considered what you have to offer. Thank the person courteously, and move on to an alternative. Options never cease to exist, although the gap between contemporary artists and venues is getting wider by the day.

The people involved with exhibiting and promoting art get the same treatment by many, as the artist gets from anarchists and critics. First and foremost, these people are also viewers, and should be treated with respect. More often than not, they have responsibilities to others and an agenda they must follow. They are not making decisions about your work on the same basis as a judge or jury; they are making judgment calls, guided by the agenda they must follow. For many venues, it is not about putting on an exhibit, it's about the agenda they believe in, regardless of whether viewers show up or not; although, the stated purpose is always that there is an audience for their agenda. It is necessary to make a direct connection between what they are looking for and what you offer before you have serious discussions. Their directives are as varied as your imagination and often, their agendas are heavily laden with influences that are too numerous to isolate. Also, they work on schedules that are many months ahead, and on a daily basis they have to think in the past, present, and future.

Understanding status with regard to obligations and influences, is a necessary step for a venue and you to be able to work with one another. Just because a venue is labeled a museum of modern art or a contemporary gallery means nothing until you find out what their agenda and influences are. Choose your directions wisely so your time and the time of others is not wasted. Often, when artists discuss their art, they don't consider all the issues involved with making or not making a connection. It is a troublesome situation for both the artist and the person they are speaking with. It is wise to state your case and leave it at that. If you are not getting direct answers to your questions, there is something wrong and you should walk away. Do not bother to find out why you did not make a connection. You have done the best you can and that's all that matters.

What you see and what you get are not always the same when negotiating with a venue. It is a two way street because you have two individuals with different knowledge and understanding, let alone histories and experience. This demands each side having to be as direct and concise as possible regarding need and offer; your status has to be equal. Your creations must fit and advance the goals of the venue, and it has to fit the financial equation. The people you are dealing with are often highly educated, under appreciated, and under paid, and they're looking for the best possible connection. The decision does not end there, more often than not, the individual you are speaking with is only a go-between with a nice title, and must get an approval from another person or a committee to seriously work with you. Also, stakeholders in the venue usually dictate what a venue will exhibit and promote. The history of what a venue has exhibited is the best example of what to expect as their agenda.

I know what I said does not sound encouraging; in fact, it can be overwhelming, and the wall may appear too high to get over. Most of the time, the information coming from the other side is limited, and you as the artist, have to make decisions with an insecure feeling.

Sometimes this is unavoidable even after you have questioned your contact further. This situation may have many innocent reasons, so it may demand a judgment call on your part. There is no doubt there are people involved with art who do not have your best interests in mind, so protect yourself appropriately. Use your knowledge of the Five Ws to gather the answers you seek from those you want to deal with. Ask the same questions of yourself to fix your own needs.

"Support the arts at any cost, even if you have to shoot yourself in the foot in the name of art."

Many municipalities have a strong desire to support the arts and create centers they call a museum, where in truth what they create is a community center offering some museum style programs and facilities. Many of these facilities teach arts and crafts for young children, have a museum store, and sometimes even space for yoga lessons among the arts, along with other pursuits to involve the community. I lived in an area where the Grange Hall included all these services during the week, a community dance on Friday night, and a church service on Sunday morning, followed by a pot-luck.

The world is filled with art looking for a spot where people can enjoy viewing it, and there are many places willing to lend space free of charge for someone to adorn their business with creative works of art. I hate to say this, but, there are all sorts of opportunities open to artists who are willing to give up anything to get their work shown somewhere.

—————

I must again mention the strong division existing between venues and artists: If you are not successful you are a risk; if you are very successful, you are in demand; and, I don't think this is a surprise to anyone.

Let me give you an example of how this works:

If you decided to request a loan for your small business with great potential you would probably not get a loan. However, if you subsequently become successful, lenders will be rushing to your door offering to loan you money at the best rates!

This same scenario plays out in all kinds of pursuits. Venues don't necessarily want to promote your art, they want art that's already successful and self-promoting. Does this mean venues are lazy? No, it doesn't. What it means is they will put any promotional efforts they have into a product that will be easier to sell to a viewer or buyer.

The thinking processes of the artist and those of museum curators or gallerists are usually very different. They need and depend on each other regardless of how they think. It is the responsibility of the artist to recognize the needs of the museum or gallery; it is also necessary for the venue to accommodate the requirements of the artist. You are partners.

Often, your conversation is the last exchange on the mind of any curator at a museum or gallery, so you have to be cautious in what you say to avoid the risk of your intent being taken the wrong way. Sometimes, this partnership is contentious due to an imbalance, and you have to consider the relationship as being professional, where ups and downs are expected. Anxiety is not a part of this business; slow as you go, precise and exacting is.

Not all creative people want to step over into the world of galleries and museums; in fact, many find it absolutely repugnant because it is a diametric opposite from their frame of mind. (This is why some artists have representatives as mediators.) This is a choice each of us have to make.

Know up front that you must hold your head high; what you have accomplished thus far has given you a new perspective on self, and raised your expectations of life. I prefer to believe when a creative person learns how to exercise their plans with the proper tools, they have tremendous internal strength and drive to be able to see their path to success. Many creators are shocked at one time or another to find they have opponents in the world of art and many of them possess a great deal of underhanded ability. Don't make the mistake of believing you are the only person with a dream; be a person with the tools and knowledge to succeed but don't allow others to take advantage of your good intentions.

The end result is beyond the control of the artist; so, what we can control is exactly what we've been learning. If creating art with new materials and a technique that is beyond reproach is your goal; all the time, labor and research is your responsibility and you will receive the benefits. The hidden benefit galleries and museums provide you is a third party endorsement. Taking control and having someone take notice of your accomplishment is out of your scope of influence unless you include a plan of promotion.

Everyone wants to write the conclusion to their experience in art and sometimes you can do exactly that. However, this is the one chance in a lifetime. There are contemporary artists who have created their own destinies and succeeded by promoting their own art and soliciting craftsmen and venues to collaborate with them. But, not everyone can be a P. T. Barnum (of circus fame).

I will say, "To control the marketplace by promoting outside normal channels does not make your art better than it is, it just makes you a better promoter."

chapter twenty-one

MONUMENTS AND OPPONENTS

Here are some philosophical points of view: The unaltered line that accommodates Mother Nature to get to your goal should not be interpreted as the straight line. If you were to climb a mountain, you would be going this way and that way around trees and boulders, zig-zagging up steep slopes to get to the top of the mountain, and doing the same coming back down. As an artist, you will meet up with many obstacles and obstructions which you will have to face. Accept that humanity is made up of the past, present, and future, and those who belong in it. Your place is only temporary. You are always in motion to accomplish one goal after another; in human terms, you are comforting and nurturing humanity. The antagonist to humanity and its existence, can be likened to the straight level road, cutting through every hill and filling every canyon to get you from one place to another as fast and with the least deviation possible. If the antithesis to the straight line is considered chaos, then the straight line must be brain dead because the mind is fed by chaos. Humanity cannot look in the mirror and believe they see a digital machine that's part of the societal assembly line, unless our spirit is lost. Look in a mirror and you will only see yourself, it does not change unless you are brainwashed to believe you are something or someone else.

"Because you are an artist does not mean you are artistic."

Thoughts to advance your art germinate from a variety of different views that give you an advantage. If you were to begin to play a game of chess with a computer and you made predictable moves, you would never be able to win. If you make unpredictable moves from the beginning of play, your chance of winning is considerably better. Thus, as an artist you must constantly seek the unpredictable to better your plan of action.

Ask yourself, do we really need a monument in the middle of a forest to compete against Mother Nature with all its beauty and magnificence? Art is very personal and belongs in personal spaces where it can display its individuality and the deep meaning of its personal story, not where it invades and disturbs the natural environment. Art is not meant to displace what nature has provided.

Painting and sculpture have never escaped the private space called the cave. We often forget that we are organic and when you look at the beauty of our earth, you see a part of yourself, living and breathing in the same existence. When you look at art outside of personal space, you see the arrogance man and society impose upon Mother Nature and humanity.

———◆———

Not every artist is a person of good intention. Those who perpetuate graffiti and force it on humanity in public places are simply anarchists and vandals. Who, without responsibility for their actions, want to impose on others to bring about confusion with their propaganda. If legal permission were granted in those public spaces, it would be considered public art and there would be people held responsible. Those people would have the burden of qualifying the art and accepting the consequences. Cities and towns all over the world have been visually destroyed by these people who have no respect for the law or their fellow human beings in perpetuating their own self interests on public and private property.

What I've said is not meant to impose on you or your thoughts; I'm reminding you where ethics stand in the real world. The act of graffiti has always been a problem for humanity. The more this graffiti society and its demands encroach on us with their particular brands of equality and circumstance, the more separated we become.

Like all worthwhile endeavors, art is a competition between an inventor and all the influences, agendas and behaviors of people who want creations they support to win in the open arena. Because artists are universal creators, we have to accept that there will always be negative opposition to every positive behavior you have. This opposition has to be overcome by positive action in favor of the artist with logic, reason and understanding.

"If I can't be a part of your group, I will try to destroy everything you stand for."

The whole world is filled with people who have desires and what they are willing to do to get what they want at the expense of others. Often the means to their end is illegal. This is where competition steps in to settle the dispute; let others decide what they want to support and defend as viewers in the open arena. There are many avenues for art to reach the viewer without damaging our environment or the work of other artists. True success can only be measured by how you accept the results of your challenge.

The irony is that most graffiti artists have a common affliction, being anti-acceptance, until they're invited in. So, the act of graffiti may just be a childish way to display anger and jealousy without admitting it.

Remember also, the use of graffiti as a political statement can be damaging. And, can be used as a sign of power and control of an area like wild animals marking their territory with urine.

——•—•——

Don't use any excuse for failure. Life is about making the most out of our existence, not looking for the straw that breaks the camels' back. Everybody exists in this world with a different physical and mental plan which is out of our control. Each of us has to make the most out of our assets to succeed. It is a human condition to be habitual and susceptible to failure. Conquering those weaknesses with a strong will to succeed is an overwhelming feeling as you apply the Freedom in Art.

There is a dangerous mindset you have to be aware of and it is embodied in two words, "If only." Consciously or not, these words create more problems than is imaginable. They give great hope and at the same time put you on your knees in a desperate belief a miracle will save you from all your troubles in finding success. Truly, if you allow the "if only's" to control your career, you might as well start chasing rainbows because neither one will ever get you to your goal.

There is no plan in this book that relies on miracles. The artist's job is simply organized work with a plan to accomplish a goal. This mindset allows you to concentrate on the important issues of technique in your path to get there.

"You see, peanut butter and jelly finger sandwiches are just everyday stuff, until you dip half of each one in melted chocolate and serve them for dessert."

chapter twenty-two

WHAT DOES "SPECIAL" MEAN

Getting caught in a torrential downpour; the rain was warm and the sound was overwhelming. You couldn't keep the wetness off of you (even with an umbrella, if you had one). The moment was exhilarating, exciting, and over the top. The first thought was to run for shelter even though there was no danger. You laugh when you get out of the rain and feel like you've been saved. Saved from what? You have experienced a most exciting event which has brought you closer to Mother Nature in a unique way. This doesn't happen to you every day, and the feeling is special!

When Paul Cezanne brought his paintings to Paris and showed them to his friends, they knew his art was special because they had never heard the words he spoke (to explain his stories) from anyone and they could see exactly what he was talking about. He had ferocity and every area of his canvases had design and rectilinear forms. He did not think his art was out of the ordinary because he was enveloped in it every day. (This is a matter of perspective for the artist, being in a compartment and working; often, your inventions become useful to you rather than the special they are to the public.)

Usually, the questions asked by a practicing artist/viewer are about another artists' techniques. They somehow feel every artist should share their individual and unique style and how to create it. Absurd!

Go home, practice and invent your own tools and techniques. Imagine meeting the artist Damien Hirst and asking how he produced his shark in a tank art? Or, how about asking Jeff Koons about the process necessary to make his stainless steel balloon sculptures? Really, many artists have a very low level of pride and esteem for their behavior. But, I'll tell you this, how you put your art together should be as important to you as the iPhone was to Steve Jobs, and don't ever forget that. It is nobodies business how you create your style or technique; that is a big part of what makes your art special.

Special means particularly good or exceptional, rare and unique. What do these words tell you? All of these words can apply to one painting that would be the hallmark of a new style of art. The reality is: special paintings have a single definition like rare or exceptional with the possibility that history may elevate them later. Very little happens in art on the spur of the moment.

Most people don't recognize something as special unless they are shocked into it; thus, the need for art that breaks a mold. It takes a person with a strong sense of worth and knowledge to identify and promote art they find to be exceptional. The background story of that art is essential for them to put a label on a work as "Special" and promote it as such.

The most unique living creature on earth is a human being, and this may be why people have a hard time putting any label on a work of art, when each and every one of us are unique and individual.

Think of a diamond in the rough, which mostly looks like a piece of fractured glass. If identified, it is rare and exceptional, until someone recognizes it and it is cut to show its brilliance, which would then make it special.

Art is not a world unto itself, it needs to have a place where it belongs; it needs to have space where it comes alive and has elbow room. When you are surrounded by art (even in the personal space) you have moved the humanity of art into the social narrative of art. Living in art is like being under the influence 24 hours a day. That experience is not special, it is overwhelming. There is an exception: If you are a collector of art and expose your collection through artistic venues, that's understandable and admirable. Moderation in how we live with art may be as important as how we raise our children.

When a viewer makes an emotional connection with a work of art it becomes special to them and should be treated as such. The more unique and special you consider a work to be, the more balanced expanse of space it should dominate.

If you had a great deal of money and converted all of it into dollar bills, and filled up a swimming pool so you could swim in your wealth, it wouldn't mean very much. Even though each dollar bill has value, it is no longer special because the meaning is among a multitude of others.

You, the inventor of art, are the only person who is there from the beginning of a creation until its conclusion. It is up to you to begin the journey of identifying your work as special, if indeed you believe it is and have all the facts to justify your words.

Vincent van Gogh produced art he believed was special but he had no idea how to promote it. After he and his brother Theo died, his sister-in-law Johanna van Gogh-Bonger, then only 29 years old and with a one year old child, decided to put her heart and soul into promoting Vincents art and correspondence with her late husband. She believed deeply in the art and made it the success it is today because she knew it was special.

"If there were a single answer to the question of success, we would not be human with all our weaknesses and aspirations."

———◆◆◆———

There is no doubt, creating a work of art (even if it is unique and exceptional) is only half the journey to success. We can't discount the fact that society places an agenda on art; but these are expected biases. All we can reasonably ask for is the right platform to present our work and hope we are in the right time and place. You not only have to strive to be the best, but you also have to learn how to promote, because promotion is the other half of an artists life.

There are a few scenarios (that are available to every artist) where an artist can claim success in getting art to the public:

- First, the artist has exceptional and unique art and an individual who can promote it.
- Second, the artist has art and a very good and well known individual who can promote its attributes.
- Third, you have art and you are an exceptional promoter.

In the last category you will find two artists: Mauricio Cattelan and Banksy. Through their promotional acumen, they have had success but they have also worn the public out with stunts that have little to do with art. Will what they have done prove the test of time? Your guess is as good as mine.

Truly, the point is: Even if you are an exceptional self-promoter, every artist needs someone who believes in them and is willing to promote the art they produce. Venues as well, need to do their part in promoting art (without bias).

chapter twenty-three

TECHNIQUE AND STYLE

The most compelling technique is shock value: Something that has a sudden and disturbing effect on a viewer's emotions and may tantalize and outrage, or even horrify. You've heard the saying: "I'll know if I like it, when I see it." Many viewers unknowingly wait to be smacked in the face with a reaction to an art piece (and then they'll know they have seen it). This is the reason many viewers enjoy art with shock value. We've all seen the movies that begin with explosions, gunfights, exciting car races, or a steamy sex scene. These types of emotional techniques are numerous within the art world. Most new movements and styles have been introduced and established with an emotional impact; they are welcomed and liked by many people because it appears to make the art new and daring. There is always a new crop of young minds, who are unaware of history, and the shocking is exciting to them. You have to accept it as a part of the art experience, because it will always have a ready audience, especially when they are uninitiated. The problem comes later, after all the bombs go off, and the shockwaves have emotionally knocked everyone over. What do you do for an encore? Does anyone care? Maybe the answer is no. That's when the next bombardment is scheduled, to begin a bigger set of shockwaves to overwhelm you.

Take notice of a different aspect: a volcano is much more interesting than a mountain (although a mountain may have been created by a volcano), because in the present tense a volcano has tremendous shock value, it is thrilling and has lots of drama. Whereas, a mountain is just one of many other mountains.

———◆◆———

Artists are always looking for new techniques. There are millions of people around the world involved in artistic endeavors. Are they all looking for a new technique as the basis to fulfill a need, or to gain notoriety and success? Maybe they are. That seemed to be the historical basis for success, and most notable artists, certainly had a distinctive technique or style. Shock value has a pattern of being shocking only when the topic at hand, at a specific time, is either taboo or forbidden.

Art has developed to the point where it can be difficult to find new techniques. There are two ways someone can view art; through the eyes of technique or style. If you paint a straight line on a canvas with one stroke of the brush, that would be called technique. If you allow paint to flow down on a canvas to create a line, that is a style. If you go down the street skipping, technically you are walking with style. Going further, any distinctive or recognizable way in which an act is performed is also a type of style. If you dance while cleaning the house, you have style. You can see the difference between style and technique and how individual they can be.

There are many paintings reviled on their first showing that have become the sentinels of famous movements. So, do you as a creator have the connection to a new technique or style; or does the viewer? The beginnings of some techniques and styles are in scandal, and others are misunderstood or repulsive. Often, human nature intervenes at first glance, because the viewer has become complacent and is repelled. They have been trained to like what they have been used to seeing and cannot recognize something new. Later, after further exposure they will discover the new and embrace it, although reluctantly. Some people don't stop at this junction and question themselves further if they disagree with what is considered new. This is where original avenues in art branch off into unfamiliar territory. The reality is, not everyone will like what they see no matter what you say or do.

"What you need to know about success is enough to make your head spin while you're trying to hold on in a speeding roller coaster."

———◆———

Many creators have stretched the limit of their own truth by employing assistants to help perform and accomplish their work. There is nothing wrong with this practice; you could hardly expect an architect to roll up her sleeves and do the work of building a creation from her design all on her own. Although, the practice on a smaller scale takes away from the humanity instilled in the finished work.

Self-censorship of words and artistic expressions is harder to live with because they produce guilt. Therefore, you have to examine your motives; this can often be a double edged sword. If you have expectations of fame when you create art, that's an influence. If you're wanting to become wealthy, that's also an influence.

The principles of the Freedom in Art are separate from your obligations. They will be your greatest tools and techniques, because you're in control, and you'll be able to decide who it is and what it is independently. Cleansing yourself of influences in your art, and recognizing what you have done to achieve that state, you've opened the door to having a strong purpose in life. This is a reason to exist, and the altruism to better the human condition.

Consider technique and style as a part of story as well as being an activity or display of emotion. The Abstract Expressionists certainly believed what they painted had meaning, expressed in new forms of art. There is nothing wrong in making anything in art your subject matter and giving it life through your narrative; it's as easy as transposing from representation to abstract, and the added bonus you receive is knowing there is always the possibility to discover something you have never seen before.

———•◦•———

We now have new tools to give us new ways to get from the first thought to an end result. Digital cameras and computers have changed technique and style in many ways. Their value has been tremendous in commercial applications, but fleeting in fine art; it always comes down to the viewer wanting to see the real thing. A painting has to be displayed on a wall somewhere, perhaps in an art venue or a home. A digital picture is different; it's seen as commercial because it can be reproduced a number of times with the push of a button on a keyboard. Digital reproduction is the greatest asset digital pictures have, and the proper place to show it is in a theatre, on a video monitor, printed or reproduced as a photograph.

In many ways, technological development works very well in conjunction with traditional forms of fine art. If you want to show someone a picture of your latest painting, you can send it over email. If someone likes it they may want to see the real thing. The digital picture can work as a calling card, or a sales tool; some digital methods work wonders compared to traditional methods.

There is a difference between historical techniques applied to creations and those of digital production. Paintings from the 1600s can still be seen by putting them in a lighted area. Digital art has a finite life because technology is moving at great speed. You can still view a motion picture made in 1900 by illuminating the celluloid. A digital movie made twenty-five years ago may never be seen again, unless you saved a machine that will be able to project it, or it has been transferred to a newer digital platform where it can be played on a video monitor. How long will that machine last? This is where digital art steps into the throwaway world. Art has always been an appreciating asset, the hardware of the digital world appears to be a depreciating asset, with associated benefits. Although, internet online streaming seems to be taking over the viewing of motion picture art. You will no longer be able to own it but you will be able to pay to view it when you want to.

Certainly, digital is in the process of becoming a necessary tool for traditional artists but not as a replacement for them. There is something unholy about having a huge monitor to view the digital art you have purchased or rented. Will all the arts be viewed on a monitor or several monitors in the future?

—————

We have left out the "how to" of technique and style (other than a few examples) on purpose because this is an individual, unique pursuit added by the creator of art. I have to say, there are hundreds of books written about this subject; there is no need for more. Your desire to add to the unending number of techniques and styles is what directs you, an inventor, to pursue a better world in which we live.

chapter twenty-four

THE THREE WELL-BEHAVED SUBJECTS OF DISCOVERY, PORTRAITS AND LANDSCAPES

Discovery

The benefits of allowing your mind the freedom to go anywhere it chooses without the constraints of influence is to discover something new to you. The more experienced a person is in life, the fewer in-the-present thoughts are recognized as new to them. To say your mind has thought something never to have been thought before would not be reasonable; how are any of us to know everything that has been thought before? However, what we're thinking has to be reasonable in the context of what we're trying to achieve.

It's important not to confuse the abstract with reality. Watching cartoons and seeing the outlandish things the characters do, without having any thought the characters and events are real, is a transformative experience because we know cartoons are visual fiction. If you believe you are a god on earth and your powers are so great you can do anything and not suffer the consequences, you must be thinking through the actions of the main character in your next blockbuster script to be made into a fantasy motion picture. Our thinking has to face the reality of who we are as humans and the physical nature of our being.

Understanding the true nature of the freedom you possess and putting it in proper perspective is essential to your acceptance of who you are, and the avenues that exist in the Freedom in Art. The mental act of discovery contains portions of abstract thought and reality, in what proportions we will never know. As an inventor, you have to be able to separate the two in order for a discovery to be made useful. Abstract thinking and reality belong in the same compartment, in that way, we keep our humanity and our spirit alive because we have no boundaries outside of our own making.

—————

It is time we talk about the word "production" and how it fits in our conversation. (We have already used the word numerous times.) Artistically the word is most often used in terms of a stage play or a motion picture. It's an important word because every visual art creation is technically a complete production. In the time you have with your audience, you have to impress them with a truly exciting story. What we do as artists is theater, and you are the producer, director, writer and performer of the production, all-in-one. Oh, and you are the production manager as well. You have to pay attention to every detail to make sure you relate a complete narrative. What you discover as the complete artist may be exactly what you're looking for.

Discovery happens at any time during the process of creating and telling your story. In the act of physically creating your art, you'll be at the height of your awareness to recognize something different in your production. If you can explain the discovery, you've completed your task. Most often it's not as evident as you would like it to be; it doesn't declare itself by shouting out like you would want, and it may not fit the architecture of your current project. If the "different" aspect makes you uncomfortable, clear it from your creation; think about it until you come up with something that pleases you. Occasionally, you will find a discovery is not immediately useful but something to write down for a future project. Remember what we said earlier about diverting from your plan to get to your goal; it's not a good idea.

Imagine you are playing darts and you figure out how to hit the bullseye and do it every time you throw a dart; what you have done is made a plan of work to get to your goal. Now, if you don't know how to adjust throwing the darts and you are always missing the bullseye on the lower left; the only way you are going to hit the bullseye is if you move the target to the lower left. What kind of thinking is that? Create the goal to suit the narrative? That's a performance called "seat-of-the-pants."

<hr />

Universal truths are as different as dirt and air. The arts are made up of everything good and bad in the human condition. If you ask fifty people to write a statement about life, and you choose the ten that are the least offensive (being the most impartial to the greatest number of people), you will discover the story is neutralized to the point where there's no interest in the narrative. Life is made of conflict, contrast and objection; a story should represent those ideals, and balance them with love, compassion and understanding. More of the same without a difference is not interesting.

"The basic understanding of art principles does not equal the ability to use those skills."

Not every artist has to relate so closely with the mind or senses, and not everyone can disassociate themselves to the degree we are describing. There's no power in knowledge, it can only be used as a tool. The freedom inherent in art is a path we walk not knowing how far we'll go; or how many stops we make along the way. Many of us will slip and slide, and fall down numerous times before we learn the dangers and the pleasures of an adventure. Nothing is ever complete, and we will always find an exception. After all, the exception is often something you have never thought of or considered before. We'll smile every day and know we've been on an extraordinary journey that will outlive us in every way.

Let's write a story of discovery:

What are we looking to find when we are seeking something through discovery? First, where is the action taking place, and why are we looking for it to begin with? Who is in this place? Are we looking for something real, or is it the "something" dreams are made of? Almost anything can be discovered if you don't know it's there. It might be something you can touch and hold in your hand, or something you can see or smell. Perhaps it's a thought you've never had before. Events such as these can be complicated.

Let's say the viewer is the "who," (really different) and they're making the discovery. It's an early morning on a cloudy day. Consider this as a landscape painting and the red of the sun is peeking through dark clouds. It won't be a representational landscape, but instead an abstract painting. We're going to play with the order and size of what you'll see, using the Five Ws in a different way, allowing the viewer to be part of the creation. Instead of mostly brown, with some contrast of grey and white, and a bit of dark red, we will change it to mostly dark red, with some contrast of grey and white, and a bit of brown. The canvas will be dominated by a rectangular, dark, cool red, surrounded by a necklace of grey clouds, with a rectangular sharp sided ribbon of white, and a dark blueish brown border.

We have changed the perspective of many layers into a flat focal point with dimensional layers. (This is a great time for you to think about giving your mind a workout by discovering a new technique to depict this story in a different way.)

The viewer will have to see the story in the painting with their mind's eye. The caution is that every viewer will not be able to see the meaning in your production; that's why you have to label it with a name or description to pull the viewer in. A fishing line is nothing unless there is someone there to reel it in. Human nature loves to experience discovery.

"Remember, nothing is simple except doing nothing!"

Portraits

It is not the easiest, and yet not the hardest subject to portray. The problem often comes from elimination of more than one of the Five Ws, depending on how narrow your subject view is. Artists who work on portraits often believe it's more about technique than any other aspect in the creation, and there's a lot of truth to that statement. Sometimes, the success of a portrait is more about the reaction of people than the quality of the art.

There are great opportunities to bring a story to every creation, including the portrait. You have to ask yourself if you can simulate life purely with lines and planes or is there more to it? Often, painters forget about the negative space of a portrait to concentrate singularly on the subject eliminating any depth to the character. There has to be a connection to the viewer and that bridge comes from the background space in the painting. Yes, it can be more work; but isn't that what it's all about? There's beauty and drama in everything, including the portrayal of human beings.

"Every portrait is a stereotype, including those having an individual identity."

There is a concern many of us have about identity and what it means in different contexts such as the portrait. Historically, people have used stereotyping for purposes beneficial and detrimental to their beliefs. In times of conflict the process is used to demonize an enemy in the minds of patriots. It can also be used to bolster the beliefs of a population against the enemy by characterizing themselves as better people. Stereotyping is the embodiment of everything in our identity. In the arts, almost everything you do has some aspect of stereotyping. You have to get your point across quickly and you have to express every feeling and emotion in a visual form. Meaning, you have to use lines, planes, color, perspective, design dynamics, everything at your disposal to make your point.

Stereotyping is part of every novel, story, movie, painting and sculpture. Art is not about reality; it's impossible to recreate a dog in a picture, only nature can recreate the animal. We can only create a vision that the mind recognizes as a dog. Every time an actor plays a roll in a movie they participate in the stereotyping of that character and themselves. Do not discount the tremendous benefits of the truth you create in the landscape of a stereotype, whether you model them, or create them. Demanding an identity and then complaining that it is typecasting or stereotyping is pure nonsense.

Let's make up a story and see where we can go with it:

First, let's do the Five Ws in quite a different way: Let's call a character Yvonne, who is carefree and loves to travel. When she does, she feels she is getting away from negative influences in her life that bother her. She is not a lonely woman and she is most secure with the wind in her hair. To her, it doesn't matter where she goes so long as she can breathe fresh air.

Can you see what happened here? We've come full circle and landed on who Yvonne really is. Now you might be asking, "How are we ever going to paint that?" The Five Ws tell a great story and we can make a lot out of them. We know she's free, and loves to breathe fresh air and have the wind in her hair. She appears to be an outdoors person and she's not going to the arctic. She may prefer going to warmer climates, and she feels she is never alone because there's a spirit with her all the time. Yvonne is very mystical in her beliefs.

When we think of free spirits and nice weather, we usually think of places like Hawaii, the South Pacific, Florida or Southern California where you are more likely to have beaches and warm breezes. Her adornments are a ribbon in her hair, a flower behind her ear, and a shell pendant hanging from a string around her neck. She's looking stage left (viewers' right) into the wind; the fingers of her left hand holding a shell pendant, with palm trees in the distance behind her. She is touching, sensual, alive and adventurous. In her heart she believes the wind is the spirit calling her.

In the portrait of Yvonne we have created a stereotype of a person but we identify her by name to give her an identity that's individual. This would be a great representational portrait with lots of color and light.

Landscapes

Painting foliage is a people pleaser, since it allows for any style you want to use, not because it's organic. There are groups of artists who believe Mother Nature is all you need to know about the subject of a landscape, and the rest is simply academic. They plan their entire careers on the beauty of their landscape paintings. These beliefs are not unique to landscape painters, it's just more generalized to them. In every subject we have talked about, there's a group who idolize the subject, put it on a pedestal and nothing else matters.

You have to believe every scene has a soul; that it has an identity that needs to be exposed to the viewer. Representation is fine; however, there's always something telling you the rest of the story. The various colors of a hill may tell you what time of year it is; diagonals may interest your eye and indicate the direction the artist wants you to follow to get a full view. The trees, the grasses, the rivers, the animals and atmosphere, all have something to say. Think of the landscape painting as a portrait of Mother Nature. Sometimes there are deep dark secrets in the depths of a forest. Also, broken clouds allow sunlight to be a dappled touch of color on your scene.

—————

Many artists begin their careers painting landscapes for the obvious reasons: the subject is forgiving and the principles can be bent without the structure falling apart. What more can you ask for?

Take one step further and make the landscape sizzle: add the human touch. Give it a measuring stick by putting a human being in the picture to give it scale, which is the "something" missing from the landscape and is best represented by a figure everyone can identify with. By doing this, you will immediately put a focus point in the creation and everything else adds beauty.

chapter twenty-five

TABOOS

There are innumerable unspoken "dangers" in society that make it hard to choose examples without violating universal trust. This is seen most notably in motion picture making, and not likely in two dimensional art. Society as a whole has many weaknesses and we all have a share in protecting those trusts. We traverse through these weaknesses every day without a second thought as to how important they really are. If we were to unlock these and promote them in destructive ways, all we would be doing is promoting everything that is NOT sacred and constructive for humanity and society. Even the most successful writers of horrific stories don't violate these taboos.

"Horrific crimes are those that change society."

In a free society we have universal trusts, and we have laws. Every day we encounter situations where a universal trust is exposed and puts us or others at risk. Many times we intervene or call the police to settle an issue, and in so doing, we strengthen universal trust. The Freedom in Art has responsibilities as well as the freedom to conceive anything one would want. Universal trust is in effect, however not in every situation. We, as a people, make amens for some universal trusts and learn all the weaknesses and respect them and how they must work without a second consideration. There are boundaries in these weaknesses that none of us violate consciously. Simply speaking, if you purposely break the law, you have violated a universal trust. If this happens in a horrific way, that would require changes in our lives, challenging our constitutional rights of freedom.

chapter twenty-six

THE FREEDOM

The issue of where the Freedom in Art fits into all art is loaded with individual likes and dislikes. Frankly, it doesn't matter what your subject is, or what style or technique you use; if you base your creation on a foundation of strong subject, story, and the Five Ws, you'll have a better outcome, and you'll be able to explain the reason for your work with a more fitting response; that's where the Freedom in Art principles fit perfectly.

The spiritually unblemished blank space is an unconditional example of the Freedom in Art. Anything added or subtracted bends principles into something else which may be reclaimed by the degree of integrity held by the creator of art. Since art is in the eyes of the beholder, the freedom only exists when the artist and the beholder agree. It is the gracious nature of the Freedom in Art that makes the philosophy as strong as it is. Without exception, the beliefs this philosophy promotes, brings together all the best qualities of every style and movement. This foundation must have an identity that is unquestionable, otherwise it will not stand the test to prove its value in the art world.

Attaching the Five Ws to a subject that is of a universal nature carries the risk of it being labeled propaganda or worse. All creative activities are included in the Freedom in Art. The importance, is that you are now able to recognize each creation for what it is and you can make judgment calls as to what is appropriate and objective. Many artists have produced works whose only foundation is the influence of something that cannot be qualified. Most of these works are static images that do not have a story, only an agenda. Be that as it may, many artists using these agendas, wrongly use themes that are of a universal nature and cannot pass the "yes or no" test of individuality. To say all people of a certain political view are honest, or a specific race of people are stronger than any other is inaccurate and distorts the facts. On an individual basis you can say you know a person (from a certain country) who has proven to be very honest, or, some of the best baseball players in the world come from such and such country because you know by experience and fact, the statements are individual, truthful and not applied to a general population.

The Freedom in Art gives you the freedom to defy expectation and glory. There are no rules, but there are guidelines on how to go about it. In addition, you have to convey passion within your creation to show you have the love for it.

———✦———

Do paint brushes and palette knives know they are at the beck and call of an artist? Of course not; they are tools. We have to be intimately concerned with the belief inanimate objects carry the thoughts, and ownership of the user. To understand the Freedom in Art, you have to accept that you, as a creator, have given yourself willingly to the freedom to create. Your tools will never know the color of your skin, your gender, your religious beliefs, your culture, your sexual preferences or the shape of your nose. You control those influences, they don't control you.

When you are given change from a purchase at the grocery store, do you question who handled that money since it came into general circulation? That money is a tool having no attachment to who or what you are.

When the word freedom is used there is confusion as to the definition or meaning. Many people believe freedom means you can do whatever you want, and get away with it. This is not the meaning as it is used in this book. The word freedom does not mean a person is without the responsibilities and consequences attached to art involving two or more people. The Freedom in Art has an identity and a purpose that is expressed in its goal to add to the human condition. Thus, each believer has to have this purpose in mind. And, there are a set of principles to follow which are designed to direct you to the final goal objectively.

The Freedom in Art demands certain behaviors in order to be free. You have to cleanse yourself of many inner and outer influences, and you need every tool, style, and technique available to create your work of art. That's not too much to ask. Those who want to change the fundamentals of art away from the Freedom in Art and the open competition platform, are the rivals of all art and artists.

Can you betray your own principles? You do have to compartmentalize and give up much to accept the Freedom in Art. The necessity for common ground is instilled within you. You are the common ground. You are the author and understand all of the ramifications and purposes of relating a story.

———◆———

The artists Michelangelo Caravaggio (1571-1610) and Vincent van Gogh (1853-1890) had the freedom to compartmentalize their art despite having very troubled personal lives. Although Caravaggio was convicted for his involvement in two duels with daggers and swords that resulted in the death of at least one of his opponents, he was still able to return to the compartment and produce stupendous paintings. He had a profound influence on the Baroque style. Vincent van Gogh was institutionalized twice after having mental breakdowns. The second time, (in which he volunteered to go to an asylum), he continued to work and even to paint outside of the institution. During his time of treatment he was able to produce a tremendous number of paintings.

When you're not creating or thinking about art, you can be whatever you want to be, and have the freedom to hold whatever principles you desire. Remember, when you are in the compartment, you are telling stories that have been created by you from many sources of reason, knowledge, and research that you have put a lot of effort into. This is not a deep rooted psychological game. This is a process where the artist has to put themselves out to produce a complete production with all the bases covered. The final result will be art the inventor knows every facet of; its creation and existence, rock solid. People in many walks of life have compartmentalized in their given fields and when they step out, they can have all the foibles and insecurities anybody else can have. You can also have the security, self-confidence, and strength of knowing exactly who and what you are. This allows the artist to search deeply into the techniques they want to use.

Many artists believe they have a conversation with their creation during the production stage. Maybe there's more in that feeling than is displayed on the surface. There is a need for the artist to make a connection with the story, like being a singer in a band where each instrument has to be working with other instruments to get the song across the way it should be presented by the singer.

chapter twenty-seven

MUSIC

What we call music is the art of sound and silence, and it can be found in every corner of humanity; it is therefore considered a universal truth. The art of music is closely related to the structure of painting. Many visual artists have known this relationship, and have associated the principles of painting with music in one way or another. Do we see melody and harmony in painting? Is there such a thing as rhythm in art? How about the dynamics of lines and color in a painting? These elements can be found in all the arts by sublimating one aspect for another. There are as many different styles of music as there are styles in visual art. The relationship in structure is most important. Most music has a subject, a story, and the Five Ws like a well balanced painting only the technique used to describe the deeds are different.

How many times have you heard of a singer saying how surprised they were when a song they thought was weak became a million seller and the song they thought would be the hit came to nothing; it happens all the time. This is evidence of a detachment between the creator (writer) and the performer. However, the public is your audience and partner, and although you're a creator or a performer, in the end, the public tells you what will be liked or rejected in any time and place.

"Even music translates into visual art."

Recognizing a song from years ago playing on the radio, I went to the internet to see if I could find a video of the singer performing the song. I found the video I was looking for and also found several well-known singers who performed the song. I listened intently to the rendition that became a hit and then listened to the others. Admittedly, I was disappointed. The only rendition that touched me was the one that became a hit, and obviously, the singer touched a lot of other people like she touched me. I'm relating this experience so you have an example of how multiple artists can have the same exposure and express it differently. To me, it was quite evident the singer who made the song a hit was the one who put in the effort to think about every word she was going to sing, and what those words would mean to the listener. She chose the technique and created the vocal style to make the words vibrate.

At some point in time, you have to come to the realization that you must give your all to every creation. You have to be fearless and responsible. It appears music, like visual art, is empty without an identity and technique; even symphonies have silent words to describe the meaning and flow of the music.

All the arts have something to share with each other. The emotions in music come from sound and silence organized in time that include components of pitch, rhythm, dynamics and values of timbre and texture. Imagine how you relate musical qualities to painting.

chapter twenty-eight

BODY AND SOUL

Each one of us has a three slice pie devoted to life. Those slices are support, procreation and art. Some people select only one slice of the life pie and devote their existence to that endeavor (such as support) and leave the other slices of the pie to somebody else. This is a shallow life that few people choose for themselves. Others desire a more varied life and settle for two slices of the life pie (maybe support and procreation). Still, there are those who want all there is to have in the whole life pie (support, procreation and art). You can mix and match these slices any way you want, including sub-dividing each slice into smaller pieces allowing dominant and subordinate interests to reflect an individual's lifestyle and age.

The truth is: each one of us can be what we want to be and there is nothing that can be done about it. So, every artist can also live life as a viewer and as a critic. Does that mean we can say or do anything we want no matter in what company we keep, or what the situation may be? No, it does not mean that at all. All three of these pursuits have to be compartmentalized so you maintain control of your mind and your behavior: An artist is only an artist when in that compartment; a viewer is limited to like or dislike when in the compartment, and a critic can expound all they want to while in their compartment. You can only be in one compartment at a time or during any face to face encounter. Changing time and place allows anyone to jump to a different compartment and engage in a different interaction. You might ask why I'm telling you this? Because, this is the only way to approach confusion and move forward. Each one of these compartments have different needs and to debate all of them at the same time only adds to the uncertainty that already exists.

⸺◆⸺

We need to put some additional thought into what we are doing by having a deeper conversation about what it is to be an inventor. By this we mean being a person who originates a new way of thinking or devises a new process or article.

The human mind is born with a blank slate, and it is nurtured and exposed to random thoughts. Each mind gains affinities some people would call talent or behavior which may be in its developed stage. To say all the great artists of the last 150 years only created what they did because they had talent would suggest they didn't have to work or think about what they created. Yes, we have said an artist is a person who creates to fulfill a need. Some people think this means you have to be compulsive, which it does not. There are people who are obsessive, but they are not the mainstream. For most artists it is the desire for self-expression by using a medium such as paint or the computer. Having a need does not mean the artist has to sublimate anything in their life to fulfill that need. Satisfying a need is part of the artist's life, determined by the individual's desire for expression when they feel the time is right. This desire can be isolated to the artist or submitted to the open arena in competition with other like minded people.

"All compartments have needs."

This is the challenge:
> *If you decided to be a race car driver and you were the fastest in the speed trials of a race; would you consider yourself the best driver if you were given the pole position to start the race as leader of the pack? The only*

logical answer is no, because the car was the fastest in the field and you were only giving it fuel and keeping it on the track. You are the best driver if you win the race in competition with other drivers.

What does this scenario tell you? No matter how good you think you are, that does not give you any extra standing in the art world. And you, like everyone else, have to go to the open arena in competition with other artists in a given time and place.

Here's some backstory that gives artists more drama. I'm sure you have read the stories about artists who were dirt poor and sacrificed everything to fulfill their artistic needs. Well, that conversation leads to a great deal of conflict about money and the creative process. Many artists feel they are selling out if they accept money for their creations, which appears to be an altered reality. Others feel whatever money is offered is never enough for a creation that is one-of-a-kind and will never be repeated. Some artists believe accepting money for their art is like selling their soul. These are all mental conditions many artists never get over because they have not had a sustainable foundation. Also, many stories about artists are concocted by others who have ulterior motives and influences. Truly, there is no single answer to this conflict that would satisfy anyone. And, having to decipher the truth when the principles are not there is impossible. Stories have been created that not only get your attention, but play to your feelings and emotions. First and foremost, supporting yourself is a priority and anybody can do it. You are the only one responsible for yourself and then be able to indulge in art. It would be nice to be able to afford to do art without the worry or concern of how to pay for it, but few of us have that luxury.

"Art is like water, it is very good for you, but if you immerse yourself in it too deeply, the consequences can be deadly."

We tend to forget all artists have circumstances and choices. Many have made bad choices. It's a sad commentary that often, even in the art world, success comes at the expense of someone else, who may never have a chance to bring to reality their own dreams. This points to the fact that life is, and always will be competitive. None of us can blame others for our failures if we refuse to fight for what we believe in and disregard our responsibilities. In any exchange of support for your creations, remember what the circumstances surrounding your position are. It would do no good to give away who you are and what you are for a promise. Don't forget, fools are made every day and you don't want to be one of them.

Most people believe you have to possess something magical to create. Since when have humans been given these super powers? It's just not true. Don't view unusual visions like they are magic, change what you see to innovation. Getting down to doing the process of art is all you have to do.

By now you should know the principles of the Freedom in Art. Ask yourself how you can instill the spirit needed in your creations if you have conflicts with the spirit within you? This is a good exercise for anyone. You do have to give up all the conflicts within yourself while you are in the compartment of art to be absolutely free, and to invent the best creations possible. If you are willing to give up creation after creation by erasing or wiping off what you have done until you recognize the strength of your abilities, you know you will be in control and at the top of your game. Every subsequent creation you produce will be making a testament to all the artists who have ever been, and to those who will come after you.

"Being a responsible inventor means no excuses"

Anybody who puts a pencil to paper is an artist. As long as you can direct the pencil to do something, you have accomplished the goal and proven my point. You might not think you have been creative; however, you have been. It comes from the roots you plant.

Do we have different degrees of artist? Yes, we do. You can be an artist if you only concentrate on one parameter of art such as color or perspective. You can also spread your wings and cross over into other genres like music, writing, architecture or maybe designing clothing. Your goal in being creative is to fulfill the need you have to create, not to get approval or get stuck in mental confusion. Being a responsible inventor means no excuses and no second thoughts while you're in the compartment. Your personal issues are not relevant; your commitment is demanded.

Most inventions are created when there is no expectation of pay-back. You are given a free pass to create great art. Your bonus is that you will have all the truths in your story, to give you great strength and be ahead of the game. If you want to sell your creation, go ahead. You are in control. What more could you ask for? Would you rather get paid to create for someone else and have them sign your work?

———•◦•———

Before you do anything, consider the ramifications of an out of control alternative to get to your goal: If you lived in Los Angeles, California and decided to move to San Diego, and ended up in Las Vegas, what would you call that experience? Think about this for a few minutes. You leave your house in Los Angeles and drive down the road and see a nice house on a corner and decide to turn there. You continue making similar decisions until you run out of money and gas and find yourself in Las Vegas, Nevada. Then you decide to stay there and get a job to get the money to continue on your trip to San Diego. I would call it "seat-of-the-pants" driving; you know where you want to go, but all these issues come up taking you to "who knows where," with no ability to get out, and are directed singularly by the promise in your mind to return to the issue sometime in the future. When all you needed to do, was plan your trip in advance, if you get confused or sidetracked, refer back to your map and focus on the route to get to your goal.

"Being an inventor with a plan is work."

Being an inventor of art without thinking may be called therapy to some people; watching wind would serve the same purpose. Yes, the Freedom in Art says you can do that, if you need therapy. Everything is possible in art; this allows you to contribute to the human experience. Being an inventor with a plan is work you cannot be afraid of since you know how to get there. You are the architect who draws the plans, sees the concept to its completion, and finally, walks out the front door and on to the next goal.

———————

Most of us think in abstract terms without knowing we do. Those terms may only be understood by one person, who could be you. Other terms may only be habits customized by culture. A creator has to recognize these conditions and know how to put them in context so others may understand them.

If you have contact with the public, you hear people daily who begin every thought with doubt. Or, end every statement with a question. This is quite normal in the human condition. However, if you want to create a project or production, you have to edit your thoughts to eliminate influences, and you have to know why you are doing it. If you put your thoughts in writing it is easy to then clip and paste to put them in an order that can be understood by many people. In other words, this practice will transform your thoughts from random to a solid plan to get from here to there.

I'm going to give you a slam dunk. You don't need to take small steps to be able to create. What you have been reading are simple truths called the Freedom in Art. These premises make it easy for you to leap ahead without having to take a lot of time, and micro-understanding simple truths, to get to your goal. This is not learning about Theoretical Physics or Biology. Why would you have to learn what's under the hood of a car to be able to follow the rules of the road, how to turn the steering wheel, brake, and make the car go? As you create, your research will fill in all the background knowledge you need.

When I was in kindergarten I had to sit at a table with a blue table-cloth. The teacher put a plate in front of me with three colors of paint on it and said, "Have fun." She came back to me many times to see what I had done and to look for something in my finger paintings on the blue tablecloth. She would say, "Look you painted a strawberry." Or, she would point to a figure and say, "That's a cupcake!" Imagination works wonders on humans of any age.

I've heard it said, there are two kinds of people in the world: those who know it all and those who know where to find the answers. But, there are also those who are dominantly physical people, and those who are dominantly thinking people. Today's artists have to be dominantly thinking people who know where to find the answers; you can be a physical person when you are out of your compartment. You can be a different person at different times In your life as well. You are the one who controls the spirit of who you are, and deciding to change your life by going in a new direction is up to you.

It's the story that counts. You have already seen demonstrations that explain how easy it is to gather the Five Ws, and put together a story. With this knowledge you will complete 90% of your next creation. At this point, it does not matter what colors you use, or what brush strokes you apply. Put the Five Ws together as you would any collage and you will see your creation start to come alive. Don't fret over anything, and you will be in the company of many of the great artists of the last hundred years. You are in your own compartment and your focus is absolute.

It is human nature to question ourselves and our beliefs. For some of us, it begins very early in life due to circumstances beyond our control. For many of us, it begins when we face our responsibilities to support ourselves. Thus, creating a plan to find our way in life.

The circumstances and answers individually are tremendous. The older we get, the more we have these thoughts that we are too old and time has passed us by. We have been beaten down by our experiences and we feel we don't have the energy to overcome obstacles and succeed at something worthwhile. When you get these thoughts, think of 98-year-old artist Luchita Hurtado, who now is getting wonderful acclaim for her art. We know everybody wants something and giving up on a dream only leads to nothingness.

The learning process can be likened to a pot of hot water over a fire. The pot is your brain, the water is knowledge and the fire is your desire to learn. The greater your desire of learning the hotter the fire will get and the sooner you will have to fill the pot with more knowledge. Turning the fire off allows the water to cool and thus you won't be able to fill the pot with more knowledge than it already has. Learning has only two options, either you are learning or you're not. Your age does not tell you when to stop work, your body and brain will take care of that when the time comes. Take note, unused knowledge does not last long in memory. And, if you have the ability to understand what I just said; you have a lot of work ahead of you and a lot of goals to plan for.

chapter twenty-nine

HOW WE SEE

Until now, we have been defining the Freedom in Art in general terms. It is time for us to examine the lens we've been using so we can come to a broader conclusion. The need to do so separates the organic nature from the pure objective nature of what we see.

No eye-witness account will ever read exactly the same as another, unless you have been behind the lens of the camera, and what is out of view of the beholder will never be seen. Thus, every creation is not the complete picture of what we see in real-life. Thinking and seeing are disconnected so your perception is distorted. This is why chronology is important to tell a story. The sequence of events in an artistic creation have to be compressed into a time and space of one minute or less; and, within that view in time, you must display as many of the feelings and effects of the five senses as possible.

We are organic beings, and we have limited abilities in the real world. Objective truth is only as good as our ability to gather it by using as many sources as possible: our senses, mechanics, and our mental understanding. This is much different from what we discussed earlier under the heading "The Mind's Eye and Basic Understanding." What you see in the mind's eye is governed by who you are. How we see is the expression of the mechanics of what you are and report. You can say it's the difference between subjective viewing with two eyes, and objective viewing through one lens.

Understand, we are talking about many different parts of physics when we express how we see: the dynamics of color, lines, shapes, and, even weights and measures. Some people disregard the physics of how we see because their mind is focussed on an influence unrelated to art. Even when you explain the physics, they will never accept the facts. The way you place lines and shapes can give you perspective, anger and sweetness. Black recedes like a black hole sucking in all color and light, and white advances like the sun ejecting all color and illumination. The weight of colors in relation to one another give you balance. Color can even give you warmth, calm or a cold feeling.

Admittedly, two eyes are not as exacting for visual art as one lens. The problem is, at any given time, which eye view will be used in a production. The stereo effect of the picture we see with two eyes wide open gives us two views the mind uses as a tool for depth perception. This is why most visual directors carry a lens hanging from their neck so they can see exactly what will be portrayed. That is why one lens is objective.

chapter thirty

WHAT HAS HAPPENED AND WHERE DO WE GO FROM HERE

Everyone has different beliefs. Releasing the tension between your beliefs and those of others is an action of great importance; some would also describe it as releasing the hang-ups you have. Respect the beliefs of others, because it is the right of every human being to believe as they wish, even if you see problems in those beliefs. It's not up to you to correct them and convey your beliefs like a prophet. If you are asked, you might share depending upon the situation. These words are to remind you to be magnanimous. Viewers can read anything they want to in your creation. You can see this behavior applied to numerous paintings of the past in the never-ending academic guesswork of trying to figure out the trust meaning of a creation.

Believing in the Freedom in Art is your mission. These are belief trusts, not laws. We have to believe in these core values in order to envision our goals and objectives. We have to be willing to stand for the truth in whatever way possible. Sometimes that means we should not be nice in our argument, and we have to step in the mud. Don't look for a fight; however, you should stand up for yourself when the time comes. And, we need to build our inner strength when we know we have the reasoning to overcome and succeed. Never changing the subject, because you'll risk lengthening the argument, and possibly make your point ambiguous. In other words, you have to know when to back off or stop. One issue at a time is the rule, and don't make it personal.

It seems intentions are more important than appearances. There will always be someone who will understand the subject and the story, only to never be able to see it in your creation and vice-versa. Simply, not everyone has the ability to learn the language of art, no matter how many times and different perspectives you offer. Many artists prefer to let the viewer see what they want to see simply because you can't be all things to all people. This, of course, is the exception to the rule.

Listen to artists and sales people talk about art, and from many you will hear confusion. While many styles are part of an objective movement, artistic explanations are usually personal and tend to be more metaphysical or spiritual. What bothers me the most, is many artists and sales personnel appear to be intelligent people, who think by making their speech complex and hard to understand, it gives them an authority that is talent driven, and above the scope and knowledge of the listener. How wrong they are. The listener is a willing partner, and has to be respected as an equal. The best policy is to use language that is the most acceptable to the greatest number of people. We have to accept that someone with a master's degree will be able to comprehend every word you speak; and we also want to know someone with a high school vocabulary will as well. Don't think this declaration is about being unsophisticated; the most important aspect is focusing on your audience, be they one person or a room full, who will be able to understand you. By using easily understood language you will accomplish your goal.

We've been speaking about a foundation in art that gives you a strong story to tell as part of the Freedom in Art. It's the spirit of creativity that has been used by humanity for everything you can think of. It's the object of all that is good and bad, and the reflection of the human condition.

The argument about talent versus knowledge has always been a contested one, and it wanes back and forth because they both have a point to make. What has to be asked is: "What makes an artist?" Can an artist be talented without the knowledge of how to use tools and mediums to assist the talent? Or, can a college graduate in art history have the immediate ability to paint great art? Whichever side you champion, you must have respect for the other side as an equal. It's a difficult position to be in as an artist; you're constantly being addressed from every direction, and by every influence disagreeing with the freedoms embodied in you. This is an argument that has no resolution, and to engage in it only creates a wider divide. Stand tough, be kind, and stay objective.

It seems to be a great concern of some people to ask, "Why do artists create?" As I have said, it's to fulfill a need. In addition, there is a philosophy to attach to this answer as well. The purpose of our existence as inventors of art is to add to the human condition. The history of humanity has formed what we have in the present; what we are doing today, is the foundation for those who follow us in the future. It is an organic experience with a noble cause. I don't know anyone who willingly admits they want to hand a broken home and foundation to future artists.

———◆◆———

Those of you who believe in the Freedom in Art and the Five Ws, should apply them using yourself as the subject. This application will give you an identity, and attaches you to the principles of your belief as a partner. Like a marriage, you'll change in time and you'll have to reassess yourself again and again. As we grow in life and knowledge, our wants and needs organically change as well. We have to recognize those changes, and work with them so we can fulfill our mission. You will have to have trust in your mission as a believer, and you will then join a movement of like minded artists and viewers.

Being creative should never supersede your obligations in supporting and procreating. This is a three slice pie, it evolves into different size portions during your life and it should never be forgotten or discarded. Each portion has its own wants and needs at different times, and you will have to exit one compartment and enter another with your full agreement and confidence as needed. That is how you survive and everybody is happy. Other individuals in your life have to understand your needs and desires as well, and you must come to terms with theirs.

> *I need to add a powerful thought here: If you live an "A" life and a "B" life, sharing your "A" life with some and your "B" life with others, you are forcing your friends and loved ones to take sides. They will only care about the side you share with them. They will have no feelings and no reason to care about the side you do not share with them, though in times of crises, you may feel they should. The life you do not share will end up being the "whatever" life. Remember, half a life is no life at all.*

———◆◆———

We have talked about asking difficult questions to create a story, and changing style from representation to the abstract. We accept the two dimensional creation as being a picture, unless the action is moved into two or more frames which creates a cinematic experience. We know all avenues of two dimensions haven't been completely explored. The nature of two dimensions leaves us with the reality of using technique to give the illusion of three dimensions and adding the spirit that makes the subject sing, besides knowing you can see it and touch it.

———◆———

"There Is no end to exploration, because in reality, it is only the beginning of discovery."

Is it your intent to create new worlds in art that will thrust humanity into a new realization of who they are and what their purpose in life may be? I know some artists who believe this is the only pursuit that's worthwhile for the modern artist. They spend all their time thinking and creating what they believe is the future. It's very difficult to wrap your brain around this notion because none of us know what lies in the future. You can surmise what might happen or guess what might come true and you are skirting on subjective opinion, that's all. The farther into the future the depiction is, the more outlandish the scenario will be. Otherwise, you are not even making an educated guess, you are simply dreaming and hoping the "what if?" might materialize. This is "seat-of-the-pants" thinking and an exercise akin to writing fantasy; it does have a place in art. However, the purpose has to be clearly understood to be a work of fiction and the Five Ws must be believable.

Example:

Think of Mary Shelley's "Frankenstein story," it would never have captivated its readers if they had not believed the narrative could be true as of the day they read the story in the early 1800s.

This is where the switchback exists: the end is the same as the beginning. The farther in the future you project, the more abstract your thinking has to be. Think of a puzzle with a conclusion, you start putting it together with the first abstract piece and continue finding pieces that fit into the puzzle. Sometimes, you find pieces that fit together but don't necessarily match your previous discoveries but you continue with your search. Finally, you piece together all of your discoveries and you have arrived, not at the end of discovery but at the middle point where it is representational and is something you understand in the present because you know the Five Ws. Now, turn the puzzle over so you will not be influenced by this reality. From this point into the future, the discovery process subtracts pieces until we lose comprehension of what is reality and we end up at the beginning again with a singular discovery which is abstract, unpredictable and begging to be understood. It is now up to the artist to use subtracted pieces to formulate a new reality with facts, not the same reality. Thus, you have never gone beyond the knowledge you already have, giving the viewer the belief your discovery is true in the present.

The process you just read is direct and to the point. In reality, you don't know how many abstract pieces there are for you to add or subtract, you only know the scope and size of the puzzle in front of you. And, every piece has a "yes or no" attached to it before it can be used or left in place at that time. This gives every visionary artist the opportunity to seek something that has never been discovered before with chance as the mediator. You will not know what the singular discovery will be until the end of the process. Your next challenge will be to recognize all the possibilities the singular abstract holds for you and to find the Five Ws to attach to your discovery.

Looking into the future of virtual reality, we're able to see a three dimensional landscape where we can walk through it with the help of interactive software and hardware. At this stage in development, this is a singular reality.

The result raises many questions that need to be answered for the artist. Imagine going on a tour of an ancient Roman town and the tour guide stops a thousand feet from the ruins and tells you it is time to use your binoculars as you walk in a circle around the ruins because the visitor count is exploding and damaging the antiquities. Or, you can sit in the bus and watch the virtual experience on a monitor. This is a wake-up call; why bother to take a trip to the ruins if you can get the same result sitting in your easy chair at home?

How about getting into the passenger cabin of an underground hyper-loop capsule that will whisk you to another city 500 miles away in an hour or so. You are underground with no way to see where you are going. You will be able to enjoy your trip on the way there by watching a video of the terrain you are passing beneath.

Eventually, you won't need to look out the window of an airplane to see the sights first hand, those windows could be nonexistent in the future and you will have to watch what's outside on a video monitor.

Digital software and hardware may be one avenue to the future as we know it; there are doubts since it removes you from reality and puts you in a virtual world, where you can see something but you can't touch it. You won't need to go to an amusement park for fun anymore, you'll be living in an amusement park. If you ever thought wearing glasses was a pain, wait until you start carrying a headset around. This is not likely to happen.

Artificial intelligence is still in its infancy, needing to be developed into a usable tool in the hands of creators and out of the hands of engineers. The camera went through the same growth pains, and did overtake many painters. Then art took a new direction and the camera has become a necessary tool for all except a few artists. New advances in reproducing the visual has never replaced the need for the paint brush, it has only given the artist another tool to work with.

Holding on to our humanity is important for us as creators, because robots and technology cannot capture the depth of human emotion, and a machine can't improvise with new creative ideas. The Freedom in

Art displays a way the viewer can still feel the emotion in a line and the blanket of color that calms us and gives emotional warmth. The world of artificial intelligence is in a space and time composed of the past and the present; not the future. The ideal outcome to any conversation about artificial intelligence would be that it be recognized as a tool, a craft, and not as a replacement in the fine arts.

The belief everything in art has already been explored and there's nothing new to be found poses many questions. There is no doubt we are now discussing thoughts and theories that have been fully explored. Intellect has proven to be timeless and universal in the history of humanity. I say look to "find" even if you think it has been found before.

The Romans had the recognition of steam, and they had the wheel, but it was many, many hundreds of years before those two were put together to create the steam turbine!

No other artist has created as you have, and in the same circumstances. You must continue to experiment and keep searching for something new. Maybe you have already found it, but you don't recognize the uniqueness of your discovery. Perhaps you have found a piece of the whole, and you have to find the other pieces to make a worthwhile and unique discovery.

In a two dimensional world, it's difficult enough to tell one story, and if you try to tell a differing story in the same context, you'll confuse the viewer. Your audience will be forever asking what the real story is and there will never be closure. Because, you have created a dilemma that has no conclusion. Although, you can paint a panoramic sequence of events where you will be able to read the pictures one after another to take you on a trip from beginning to a plausible end as many artists from Asia have done in the past. As a guide, a story has to have a chronological order in steps that are understood from the beginning, through a middle and finally to an end.

"Art is as important to a balanced life, as a balanced meal is important to good health."

Sometime you will come in contact with someone viewing your art who will say, "That's not so." Or, "You could have done this or that." Yikes! Beware, for every good word you hear about what you do, there's someone who'll voice an objection. We call this behavior artistic anarchy. The criticism of art is not a beauty contest to satisfy people who have a need to complain. I am not offended when people do this, because many of these people are uninitiated in this part of life and they do display an interest and passion for art, although they don't express it well. Look and listen until you are rock solid in your knowledge and conviction. Do not be afraid; when your confidence is strong, you can go on the offensive and start asking questions of people who challenge your art, because these people do not have knowledge of the Freedom in Art, or more than likely, they're lost in the wilderness looking for answers. Plain and simple, if you try to teach them your way of thinking, you'll more than likely be wasting time. As a creator, you retain the right to do anything you want. "Your time is my time," is a waste of energy and not the answer to every objection. You have to make a judgment call and decide what an appropriate response would be at any given moment and place. Art is a personal pursuit involving a great deal of initiative on the part of someone who desires to go deeper into the philosophy.

Often, when others recognize your kindness, they believe this shows weakness and they seek to take advantage of your generosity. In every situation, being of good nature and spirit does have its limitations in the word "reasonable." Time, place and audience, are very important considerations in what decision you make. Most people would spend more time explaining principles to school age children than they would with an individual adult, who has the ability to seek answers in a more appropriate setting. The difficulty in addressing these issues with an adult is the multitude of influences they have imbedded in their mind that must first be expelled to open the door to accepting new ideas and processes.

———•———

Many believe the serial narrative under the title "style" is the answer to everything in the success of art. It could be; when one work of art is celebrated and gains a large following, the public wants more, and artists are more than happy to produce more of the same for the artistic and monetary rewards. As mentioned, it's not a bad endeavor to serialize a style when you add an identity to each work and utilize the principle of "same but different."

Some artists disdain the thought of painting the same style over and over again, and rejoice in continuing their search into the unknown for the sake of exploration and discovery. These people are called eclectics, for their ability to derive ideas and style from a broad range of sources including those already used. Think of the artists of the nineteenth and early twentieth centuries who used the art and styles of the Far East and Africa. The eclectic is a pathfinder in art who tends to have esoteric thoughts and behaviors (intelligible only to those with special knowledge) that allow them to think outside the box. Overcoming the narratives of other thoughts is a great challenge to every artist, and each of us has to decide what our beliefs are and to diligently follow a path without deviating. There's nothing wrong in the study and inclusion of other thoughts and avenues; eclectics do it all the time. Pick and choose your pursuits and what you want to make use of.

Does every painting have to have a story? Many of the Impressionists did not appear to have a story. Most of them did have a subject and were chroniclers of a vision with a specific style. Paul Gauguin had a storyline he followed in many of his paintings.

When you're talking about what technical aspect an artist has contributed to art, limit yourself to that discussion. Many times it's a one-sided conversation from the viewer and often it's ambiguous. Look at the art of Paul Cezanne (mentioned earlier). Many artists named him as an influence in their art, and each had a different style, which in turn means each had a different visual experience. Did they listen to Paul Cezanne explain his art? Maybe they did, and maybe not.

Of all the artists I have studied, Cezanne was the most complex for me to like and understand. It took me ten years of viewing his art to find, appreciate and understand, what he was trying to accomplish. I read every book available to me and studied every picture over and over to find examples of what I read, and also to discover what I didn't read. I'm sure my thoughts are as different as those artists of a hundred years ago; I keep them to myself, as have so many others. And, I'm happy with that conclusion.

There was a time when everything in art was representational and had something to say. Numerous artists created works that had a story, the difference being that many were staging an existing story not creating one. These were artists who were told what to paint and how to do it. They were telling a biblical or historical story using art at a time when most people did not know how to read; hence, paintings and sculptures told the story visually. This allowed religions and governments to convey what they wanted people to know. This type of art is similar to commercial art today.

As events progressed, many artists became confined in representational dogma and changed into being craft assistants rather than individual thinkers of art. Through hundreds of years artists rebelled against the establishment, and demanded to spread their artistic abilities into different styles to break out. They had the audacity to say, "There's more to art than what you've seen." And now, we're saying something similar but in a different way.

——⇥•⇤——

Is it a scene or is it a story? A scene is an incident from a story, only it's not the full story. Some artists have taken a story apart and reduced it to the principles, positioning them in full character in a setting using as much of the story as possible. A story has many parts and expresses many motives and emotions. Each part can have a separate story, such as a plot, that would serve as part of the whole. A character plays a specific roll in a story, and is essential to the narrative. If you're writing a book, you would have to take into consideration all of the parts that make up the whole. As a visual artist, you can pick and choose to compose your story.

When you add an identity to your creation, you have shown purpose in what you are doing. There's a love that permeates the creation of every artist who puts an identity to a work of art. They put an extra effort into understanding a subject and story in each and every work they complete. Even in works that have partial identity, the artist has explored every avenue of the story to get as many facts as possible without compromise; the artist takes every precaution to make sure the story is as balanced as possible.

There is a reason for everything. Thus, you may look upon what you read as the next step in learning how to build the foundation of your beliefs, and how to apply them in each project. After learning the lessons of the Freedom in Art, you won't forget them.

Understanding the nature of the Freedom in Art allows you to pick and choose the influences you want in your work of art and how to present them. There's nothing more free than the blank space; nevertheless, when you add or subtract anything, you've exercised an influence. Remember, until someone recognizes the creation, the work of art has no influence whatsoever.

Overcoming objections to what you've learned is a "must do" for you to keep a level head and stay sane. If you had decided on an education in the sciences, you would learn how the study came about, who the people were; what they found; what tools have been developed to assist you, and why it was necessary to develop the science. Then, you would graduate from the learning stage to go forth and expound on the subject with new observations and understanding. Art is no different and many of the same principles apply.

Art has to have a reason for being, meaning you have to learn where the foundation is to be able to build upon it in whatever style you use or discover. This gives you the strength to go forth to the furthest reaches of your imagination with a clear mind. In representational art, it's easy to see and decipher the intent of the artist. As more styles and movements come around, it becomes increasingly more difficult and interesting to find the story.

Before we move on, there are two issues we must discuss: What happens when you are invited into the group, and how to have the killer instinct without going to prison.

Joining the group when invited in may play to your expectations, but the intentions of the group may be different. First of all, you haven't been invited in so others can bestow praise upon you, although they will; you are there for what you can do for the group. After all, each of those in the group have done the same before you and now it is your turn. They feel better and will use you until they have what they want and then it will be your turn to do to others what the group has done to you, so you will feel better. After you come to your senses you will realize the group is only a prop that must constantly be fed for it to survive. The truth is, you will not have the time or patience to be a group member because you will have deadlines to meet and product to produce. Being successful in art means you will have more of what you experienced before you were invited in and now you have the money to afford it.

The thoughts of having the killer instinct and knowing you can kill or discard at will are very tempting to apply outside the compartment. People have a bad habit of reading words and then psychologizing what they read. When we spoke of having the killer instinct, we were talking about killing inanimate works of art that belong to you because you have the right to do with them as you please. Nowhere in the conversation did we say you can apply the principle outside the compartment of art. Having and applying the instinct in the compartment gives you the ferocity you need to give everything to your creations and be armed for any opposition. You will not have hidden weaknesses to discover and you won't have to go behind anybodies back or stand behind others who will do your bidding. You will be armed with knowledge and determination to stand on your own two feet.

THE PAINT OF INVENTION

There is a belief you're only a true artist if you work for money, and compete with other artists for acknowledgment and financial gain, leading to acceptance of your art, making it a vocation. A person who practices the spirit of art should have a universal status, whether their work is produced as an avocation or a vocation. It's hard to understand these concepts. It is more biased toward the issues of society than to humanity. When you take away these influences you are left with the pure artist.

Society has always sought to influence or use visual art in one way or another, for purposes other than the advancement of art. Political, social, religious, and financial motivation have been the primary pressures. Art is not about replacing one artist with a chosen artist in the same play to advance an agenda, it is about creating new thoughts and art that will take us into a new era of exploration, and add to the human condition. That said, there are those who'd happily say outside influences in art have made it what it is right now. Influences may have also created the current mess we have in the art world.

It should not be a surprise to anyone that collusion, corruption, influence, and money make strange bedfellows all over the world. Collusion and corruption occur when two or more people of like mind get together, to influence the outcome of an event with a pre-determined result. We have to acknowledge the existence of this behavior; it has a great influence on where the visual arts advance, and the parameters of where it exists. Where the behavior affects you and me is when it supersedes the freedom each individual creator has; to be able to create and submit art to the open arena in a free and open marketplace or venue, devoid of outside influences and agendas.

This is where the difference between humanity and society are blatantly visible. Most inventors work in an environment of absolute truth in whatever world they create. This truth usually comes from a singular human direction, whereas a deception comes from multiple biases. We have to ask ourselves if our truth comes from fact or consensus. We have to choose our facts carefully because it's easy to manipulate and abuse humanity with lies.

The world is changing to move us from an existence of the individual, to one of society and the many. Prospects for the future are not what we have known. The success of one venture directed by a diagram of movement or action of things (a computer generated Flow Chart) does not mean every undertaking will have the same success; in fact, many times the opposite occurs. Decisions to replace individual likes and dislikes with a universal Flow Chart, do not match the rhythm of life.

———◆———

The Impressionists were the transition group of artists between the old establishment and the new order, followed by the innovators who opened the doors to anything and everything possible in art. Later, the rest of the art world changed and made it difficult to find new styles and techniques.

There are vast areas of fundamental contemporary art we should notice:

- Art for You and Me: Architecture, Housewares, Automobiles, High-Tech Design, Group Design, Site Art and techniques you can live with and use.
- Technique and Style: Beginning with Impressionism and now art that expresses modern life, Kinetic Art, Sound Art, Earth Art and Internet Art are all part of the Style group.
- Art and the Mind includes: Post Modernism, Neo-Pop, Installation, Neo-Expressionism, Non-objective Art, Outsider Art, Performance Art and Video Art.

All of these movements are constantly being revised to expand or jump out and create a new movement not yet heard or seen; the list is certainly not complete. Contrary to some thoughts that art has been explored to its furthest reaches, artists are coming up with new ways of expression every day.

"The kick in the rear: artists are only half the story."

Some say the end of these changes in art came when we recognized art for art's sake, or art for art. That may sound like art has already reached its end; leaving nothing more that can be achieved in its development. It was thought to be the final act of change in the art world, that has now simply come full circle to the beginning again. We are in the embryo phase once more. We now have a whole new set of visual elements to work with, including new materials, concepts, tools, space, and shape. The public welcomes these changes because they champion the adventurer, the explorer and inventor in all of us. And now, more than ever, artists realize they are only half of the equation in art.

Humanity is like the river that alters its course to accommodate changes in the terrain; somehow, it always ends up in the ocean. No matter where art takes us, it is still art. The only difference is the manner of thinking controlling it.

We've talked about the artist having been manipulated and used depending on the bent of the viewer. Art has also been held hostage and politicized over and over again. What it really comes down to: art and the tools of the artist are universal. Once a technique or style has been released from manipulation, it also becomes universal.

Some words have been used to label a specific time period in art and may never come back or be used to further identify the future, such as the word "Modern" to label art in the late nineteenth century and the beginning of the twentieth century. What word can surpass the word Modern? Some have instead used the word "Modernism," which still has the same meaning. In fact, what is being called "Modern" is an era from a hundred years ago. Let's replace the word "Modern" and use CCE (Change in the Common Era). Also, the Paint of Invention, which resides in the Freedom in Art, lives in the ACE (Advancement in the Common Era). In any case, we have to leap-frog this confusion because we're still headed into the future in whatever name is chosen.

———◆———

You choose what you want to defend and pick your own battles because you will be the only one to pay the consequences or reap the rewards. Is this scenario different from what you thought it would be? If it is, you now realize nobody stands alone when you discuss thoughts of art that must include an artist and a viewer. You have to respect the thoughts of others and be able to determine whether their foundation is strong. This does not mean collusion; we are talking about individuals with independent thoughts, free of any agenda.

Understanding the Freedom in Art is not unlike understanding life as we know it. Others may not like us because of age, gender, hair style, religion, race, culture, the way we dress, the shape of your nose, your sexuality, etc. We weave our way through life with thousands of positive and negative influences every day, and we make decisions that allow us to exist. When most of us can do that in our everyday lives, can you easily see the relationship in the principles you've been learning?

———◆———

There are millions of artists in the world who know how to create art; but there are few who know why. What we have shown in these pages is the way to make art original, with a very strong foundation, a story, and a reason for being. When you embrace the Freedom in Art, you will always know why you create art.

Sometimes, having the knowledge of a process is not good enough. If you want to own a philosophy, you can't be squeamish about it; you have to take a leadership roll in your life habits and those of the people involved with your art.

Is there a process we have to learn to share the knowledge we have about art? There is, nevertheless, I truly believe there is a limitation in the result. You may plan everything you feel you should carry over to another, but how do you prepare the listener or viewer to receive and accept this information? It's impossible; your audience has the unknown factor of random background experience on their side with no strings attached. If I were to make an educated guess, I would say if your knowledge precedes you that would give you a 20% chance to accomplish your goal of acceptance. If you carry a positive reception of what you say, that would give you another 20%. Finally, if your audience likes what they see in your art, that would give you another 20%. That leaves 40% of the audience in question. This may leave you with the belief that the best you can achieve will never be good enough. Not everyone will like what you have to share with them. Your accomplishment is measured by the smile on your face and the pleasure of having more than you started out with.

So you see, after gaining tremendous knowledge and understanding about the Freedom in Art, all we can reasonably expect is the gratification of being able to fulfill a need. And, if you can do this, you are a fortunate person indeed. If you can accept the least, anything you receive above that is a bonus in life. Personally, I look forward to hearing the simple words, "I like it."

As I have said, it is necessary to compartmentalize the process of the Freedom in Art, this action is something you have to accomplish to keep your sanity. None of us can devote our entire lives to one compartment of thinking, that would be an unworkable commitment. Life is made up of many different compartments that flow through our existence, we would be crazy to base an entire life on only one facet of feeling, emotion and understanding.

I encourage you, as an artist, to post in your studio
the following words:

The Freedom in Art

The Five Ws

Subject

Story

We have talked about the three segments of an artist's progression. You have to ask yourself in what order these segments should be placed in your plan. Some artists have put promotion as the beginning and others have put their art at the beginning and promotion at the end. Yet again, others have put the end game first, the promotion as the second segment and creating their art last. This question of what to put where can only be addressed by how secure the artist is in their ability to perform each of these tasks.

I have said your art comes first, through the principles of the Freedom in Art. In this way, you have already created your promotional material and talking points, then you can mold them in whatever way you want into your promotional game; after that, your introduction into the competition of the open arena is set with a strong foundation. I do believe those people who change the order in the introduction of their art, have actually done everything in the correct order and then changed the arrangement, so they might gain an audience with a form of disbelief and shock value to enhance their promotion.

Many accomplished painters do improvisations wowing their audience into thinking how talented and creative they are, without them ever considering the artist had actually practiced all the moves hundreds, or thousands of times. That's why I say this book is for practicing artists.

If you haven't clearly grasped the meaning of the Freedom in Art and how it works, I will explain it in one final explosion of words: All creations come into existence and develop in a bubble. A chicken, a walnut tree, a baby, are all in bubbles and are nurtured and fed to sprout, and take on a life of their own. What you get when they are born is determined by the ingredients and knowledge contained in the bubble. In the bubble of the Freedom in Art, if all the ingredients are not there and properly fed, the end result will not be art, it will just be something else. Like we recognize a chicken as a bird and a baby as a human, so will we recognize art when all the parameters are met.

The purpose of this book has been to help build your understanding of the world of art and the freedoms afforded you. The ease of which, is not hard to understand if broken down into its component parts. A process that is easy to apply, and, expressed as the reason for being in an artistic work.

The process is a way to explain the frustration I and artist friends and admirers of art have expressed about the lack of any foundation to determine what art means as a whole, and in each individual work. If you read the theories of art advanced by many artists and their representatives, you'll walk away shaking your head in disbelief. Rarely is there a mention of the foundation that supports the art. Thus, it became my mission to find an answer to the dilemma and to do something about it.

It is my pleasure to see hope and spirit through the Freedom in Art and I trust you will see it as well.

Pssst, there is something else you should know, which is much more important: When you practice this way of thinking and doing, you will awaken your creative self and become the artist you are meant to be.

The artist Jack Priest

The artist Jack Priest was born in Los Angeles, California in 1946. He spent his first six years in Mexico City and north-central Mexico where his father was involved in the development of mining in Zacatecas State. He has spent most of his adult life in the Western United States.

Having an interest in all types of art from a young age, he began to study books on the architecture of Frank Lloyd Wright and visited several of the homes he designed in the Los Angeles area while taking mechanical drawing classes in school. His interests broadened to include regular visits to museums and galleries accessible by public transportation. He has rarely taken a vacation where the purpose has not been to visit select museums and galleries in Europe and North America. He has been a practicing artist for more than 40 years.